Introduction to Ethical Investing in India

By Siva Prasad Bose and Joy Bose

Published by Joy Bose

Contents

Dedication

This book is dedicated to all the companies in India who subscribe to ethical values and sustainable goals.

Preface

Ethical investing, also called by different names such as Environmental Social and Governance (ESG) investing, responsible investing, mindful investing and sustainable investing, has recently become more popular. Investors, particularly younger investors, are getting more concerned over the wider social and other impact of their investments and wish to contribute to positive changes in the world, rather than contribute towards increasing suffering. The highs and lows of the stock markets in different countries further give a push towards ethical investing as a strategy to identify more stable companies that believe in ethical and sustainable values and which are, therefore, more likely to be profitable in the long term.

In this book, we introduce the concept of ethical investing and consider the avenues by which investors can invest ethically within India today. We discuss green energy, various ESG and ethical mutual funds and social investing avenues.

It is hoped that this book will raise awareness towards ethical investing and inspire existing and prospective investors to invest in a way that uses their money towards the wider good in this world.

Acknowledgements

In preparing this book, the authors would like to thank Vijay Sahu for his amazing investing course from the Siyona Academy, and Chetan Dhumane for their very helpful advice about investing.

Chapter 1: Introduction to Ethical Investing

In this chapter we introduce the concept of ethical investing.

Ethical investing has gained momentum worldwide, including in India, where companies are increasingly aligning with sustainable and ethical practices. Similarly, investors too are interested in investing in companies and avenues that align with their values. Ethical investing encompasses Environmental, Social, and Governance (ESG) investing, socially responsible investing (SRI), and impact investing. This chapter introduces the concept, its principles, and the growing trend in India.

1.1 Definition of ethical investing

Ethical investing refers to the idea of investing in causes and organizations that are least ethically harmful, and most beneficial, to their employees, stakeholders and society as a whole, as well as generating a decent financial return for the investors. This may include investing in companies that contribute to the cause of education, environmental sustainability, public health, tackling inequality, tackling discrimination and other social evils and so on. It involves companies that subscribe to good corporate governance and labor practices, as well as those that are mindful and seek to minimize any harmful impact to the environment and wider society.

Alternative terms that may refer to ethical investing include responsible investing, sustainable investing and socially responsible investing. Such investments may be in various forms of investing such as stocks and bonds or other investment types such as real estate, as long as they are related to companies that meet the ethical standards and guidelines.

The management of such companies that are chosen for ethical investments should follow ethical practices generally as well as demonstrate a good standard of corporate governance.

One example of ethical investing and sustainable practices is an emphasis on renewable energy, such as in companies like Tata Power and others. Other examples of ethical investing in practice in India include ethical mutual funds, green bonds and impact investing. Aspects of ethical investing include emphasis on sustainable practices with lower risk, longer term and stable growth rather than focusing on short term profits, and positive social impact.

1.2 Environmental Social and Governance (ESG) Criteria

They also refer to investing in company shares and mutual funds that follow environmental, social, and governance (ESG) criteria. In India, SEBI's ESG guidelines and Business Responsibility and Sustainability Report (BRSR) framework encourage listed companies to disclose and improve their ESG performance, bringing greater transparency and accountability to financial markets.

Such ESG criteria may include the following:

- **Environmental**: Greenhouse Gas Emissions footprint, renewable energy, clean water, waste management, green buildings, climate change, pollution control, control of carbon emissions.

- **Social**: corporate social responsibility, labor relations, privacy and data security, gender equality, social justice, inclusive development, product safety, data privacy and security.

- **Governance**: corporate governance, timely disclosures, business ethics, ethical policies against corruption and fraud, independent board members, executive compensation, anti-corruption, treatment of minority shareholders, R&D investment in environmental and social impact.

Over time, use of such criteria by companies may result in long term profitability and improved operational performance.

Reference:
https://www.sebi.gov.in/sebi_data/meetingfiles/apr-2023/1681703013916_1.pdf

Responsible investment policy pamphlet from Axis mutual fund
https://www.axismf.com/cms/sites/default/files/Statutory/Responsible%20Investment%20Policy.pdf

1.3 ESG mutual funds

Recently there has been a rise in ESG based mutual funds in India, with many asset management companies and mutual fund houses coming up with their own ESG funds where people can invest.

Examples of ESG based mutual funds include SBI Magnum Equity ESG Fund, Tata ESG Fund, Axis ESG Equity fund, Kotak ESG Opportunities Fund, Quantum India ESG Equity Fund and so on. SBI Magnum ESG fund, for example has shown consistent good performance due to its focus on good governance and sustainability.

1.4 S&P BSE 100 ESG Index

The S&P BSE 100 ESG Index is an index of companies which is designed to measure securities that meet sustainability investing criteria while maintaining a risk and performance profile similar to the S&P BSE 100.

The methodology followed by the ESG index excludes companies working in areas involving controversial weapons, thermal coal, tobacco products, oil sands, small arms, and military contracting. There are also exclusions based on the United Nations Global Compact (UNGC).

One can get more information about this ESG index at: https://www.spglobal.com/spdji/en/indices/esg/sp-bse-100-esg-index.

Other ESG based Indian Indexes include the following:

- S&P BSE Greenex
- S&P BSE Carbonex
- NIFTY 100 ESG Index
- NIFTY 100 Enhanced ESG Index

1.5 MSCI Indian ESG Leaders Index

The MSCI India ESG Leaders Index is a capitalization weighted index that provides exposure to companies with high Environmental, Social and Governance (ESG) performance relative to their sector peers. MSCI India ESG Leaders Index consists of large and mid-cap companies in Indian markets.

More information about this ESG index can be seen at https://www.msci.com/our-solutions/indexes/esg-indexes

1.6 Companies working in ESG sectors

There is also a surge in interest in startups and established listed and unlisted companies working in ESG related sectors such as renewable energy, green technology, agritech, solar energy, waste management, electric vehicles and e-mobility. The number of startups and investments by venture capitalists in such sectors are also rising, combined with increased incentives by the Indian government for companies in such sectors.

1.7 UN Sustainable Development Goals

Ethical investing may also refer to any investment that helps in one of the United Nations Sustainable Development Goals (SDG), which include No Poverty, Zero Hunger, Good Health and Well-being, Quality Education, Gender Equality, Clean Water and Sanitation, Affordable and Clean Energy, Decent Work and Economic Growth, Industry, Innovation and

Infrastructure, Reduced Inequalities, Sustainable Cities and Communities, Responsible Consumption and Production, Climate Action, Life Below Water, Life On Land, Peace, Justice and Strong Institutions, and Partnerships for the Goals.

1.8 Shariah Compliant Investing

Other definitions of ethical investing include investing in companies that are compliant to religious and ethical codes such as the Islamic Shariah.

Some of the criteria for being compliant to shariah Islamic law include: Shariah prohibits income from alcohol, abusive drugs, pork products, gambling, weapons, etc. Shariah also forbids investment in companies that earn most of their income from interest or Riba.

1.9 Corporate Social Responsibility (CSR) Guidelines

The Indian Government Ministry of Corporate Affairs published a number of Corporate Social Responsibility (CSR) guidelines in 2009. These include six core elements, around which companies are encouraged to form a CSR policy. These core elements include the following:

- Care for stakeholders

- Proper functioning

- Respect for workers' rights and welfare

- Respect for human rights

- Respect for the environment

- Activities for social and inclusive development.

1.10 Types of Ethical investing

Ethical investing can be in any of the following forms, besides others:

- Investing in Environmental Social and Governance (ESG) mutual funds

- Investing in Sharia compliant funds

- Investing in green energy

- Investing in social investing and social finance platforms

In the following chapters we will discuss each of them in more detail.

1.11 Conclusion

In this chapter, we have explored the definition and principles of ethical investing. We also discussed ESG criteria, mutual funds, and corporate governance standards that guide ethical investments. In the following chapters, we will examine the advantages and various forms of ethical investing in more detail.

Chapter 2: Advantages of ethical investing

Ethical investing not only aligns financial decisions with moral values but also offers long-term benefits such as stable returns, lower risk, and alignment with global sustainability goals. This chapter discusses these advantages in detail and presents research supporting the financial and social benefits of ethical investing.

2.1 Long term stability and growth

One of the advantages of ethical investing is that companies that follow good ethical standards are more likely to be stable companies that produce good value for their shareholders and wider stakeholders, and thus are worthy of investing in the long run. These tend to be more stable and have lower risk.

2.2 Alignment with ethical values

Also, some investors may prefer to invest mainly in companies that align with their ethical values. Since different investors may have different kinds of preferences on what is ethical, there is no single rule to identify ethical companies. However, some guidelines, such as those related to environment and society, may be common for most people.

2.3 Quotes about ethical investing from experts

Following are some quotes about ethical investing from a few investment experts:

"Investing is not only about making money. It's also about doing well. And the most successful investors are those who understand the issues that matter and make well-informed investment decisions." - Jeremy Grantham, famed value investor and chief investment strategist of GMO, one of the first persons to start an index fund in the 1970s.

"Investing in companies that are part of the solution to the world's sustainability challenges is not only the right thing to do, it's also the smart thing to do." - David Blood, founding partner of Generation Investment Management.

"Investors need to incorporate environmental, social and governance (ESG) factors into their decision-making processes, not only to be responsible corporate citizens, but because they can have a material impact on financial performance." - Mary Schapiro, 29th Chair of the U.S. Securities and Exchange Commission (SEC).

"Ethical investing is not just about avoiding problematic companies. It's about investing in companies that are trying to create a better world." - Audrey Choi, CEO of Morgan Stanley's Institute for Sustainable Investing.

"The financial case for ESG investing is strong. Companies that rank highly on ESG metrics tend to be better managed, have lower risk, and generate better long-term financial returns." - John Goldstein, Managing Director, Head of the Sustainable Finance Group, Goldman Sachs Asset Management.

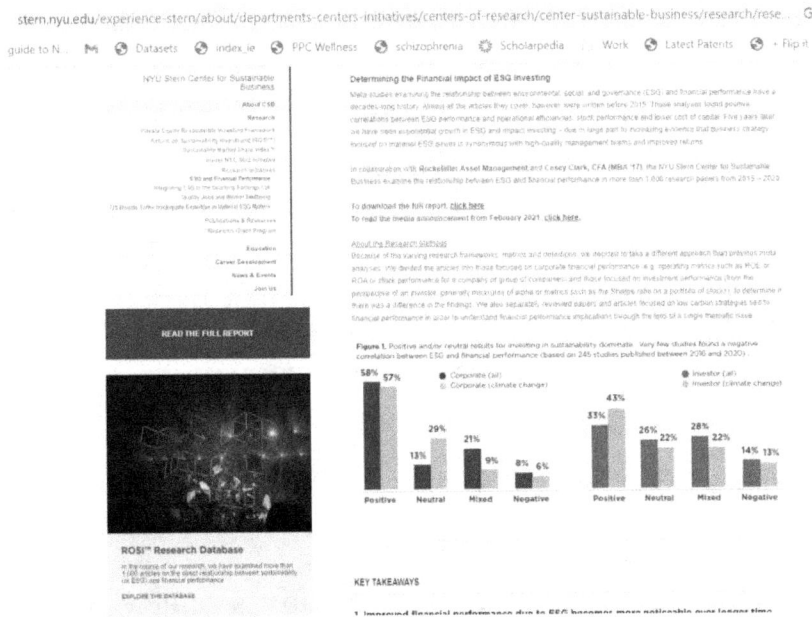

Figure: Screenshot from the Stern report showing a positive correlation between ESG and financial performance

2.4 Research on the benefits from ESG investing

The NYU Stern Center for Sustainable Business and Rockefeller Asset Management, wrote a research report on the relationship between ESG and financial performance after studying research papers written on the topic. It found a positive relationship between ESG and financial performance in 58% of their studied 1000 research papers about performance of companies (written between 2015 to 2020), that focused on operational metrics such as ROE, ROA, or stock price, with only 8% showing a negative relationship. They also found that improved financial performance becomes more pronounced over longer timelines, ESG as a strategy performed better than negative screening approaches, and that it provided better protection during a downturn.

This shows that ethical or ESG oriented investing can not only make a positive impact on the world, but also generate better returns for investment in the longer term.

References:

https://www.stern.nyu.edu/experience-stern/about/departments-centers-initiatives/centers-of-research/center-sustainable-business/research/research-initiatives/esg-and-financial-performance

2.5 Lower risks with ethical investing

If an organization is not following ESG or ethical investing guidelines, they may be exposing themselves to higher risks. Examples include the following: (from https://www.axismf.com/esg-fund-scheme)

- Companies who are generating high pollution may suffer from higher taxes in the future, decreasing their profits.

- Companies that treat their employees or suppliers poorly may suffer from bad publicity or consumer boycotts, negatively affecting their turnover and also the value of their stocks.

- Companies that have poor governance norms may be fined by the regulator.

The reverse also applies similarly. Firms that have good ESG practices will get good publicity, which means that consumers and government are more likely to look at them favorably. This is why, companies that follow ethical investing policies and practices are setting themselves up for success in the long term.

2.6 Conclusion

Ethical investing is not just a moral choice but a financially viable strategy. Studies have shown that companies with strong ESG practices often outperform their peers over the long term. The following chapters will explore different religious perspectives on ethical investing.

Chapter 3: Guidelines for ethical investing from religions: Judaism

Religious traditions have long offered moral and ethical guidance on financial matters. Judaism, Christianity, Islam, Buddhism, and Hinduism all provide principles that can be applied to ethical investing. These teachings help investors align their financial decisions with their faith. In this and the following chapters, we will go through some of these teachings and principles in different religions. We can leverage the timeless wisdom from different religions in building an ethical approach to investing.

In this chapter, we start with Judaism and discuss some guidelines for ethical investing taken from Judaism.

3.1 Jewish guidelines from Talmud and Torah

The Holy books of the Jewish people include Talmud and the Torah or the Hebrew Bible, which is the Old Testament of the Christian Bible.

General money related principles in the holy books and good money traditions include having a positive attitude towards wealth created by hard work, not to be wasteful with money, encouragement to earn money by working honestly and not by cheating or stealing.

Parts of the Torah also discourage the taking and giving of interest, especially lending money at interest. Jewish principles also include being self-sufficient about money and not depending on others as much as possible, and at the same time sharing your wealth with those in need.

3.2 Jewish principle of the five jars

This is a principle for personal finance. This is often inculcated in some Jewish kids from an early age. The principle is as follows: always divide your income into five parts in this ratio:

- 50% for necessary spending and expenses
- 20% for investing in short-term and long-term business ventures.
- 10% for savings for the future
- 10% for charity and good purposes to help others.
- 10% as an offering to God or Tithe.

3.3 Jewish guidelines for ethical investments

Jewish guidelines for ethical investing include the following principles:

- **Tzedakah or righteousness**: charity, preferably in places where donor helps the recipient to become self-supporting. The idea is that charity is a form of justice.

- **Tikkun olam or repair the world**: invest in social / environment friendly companies or orgs.

- **Tzedek or justice and fairness**: invest in companies with a commitment to social impact, combating inequality etc.

- **G'milut chasadim or lovingkindness, caring and compassion**: invest in places which support the needy, sick and elderly.

- **Tikvah or hope**: invest in places that inspire people and give hope to the world.

- Jewish ethics emphasise the duty to avoid causing harm (*hezek*). Applied to investing, this means screening out companies that damage society, exploit workers, harm the environment, or engage in dishonest practices. This aligns closely with modern ESG exclusions and reinforces the idea that ethical investing begins with preventing harm before pursuing positive impact.

- Another important Jewish principle is *bal tashchit*, the prohibition against waste and needless destruction. Today this extends to environmental harm, reckless use of resources, and pollution. Ethical investors applying Jewish values therefore favour companies engaged in sustainability, conservation, and responsible stewardship of the planet.

- Jewish teachings strongly emphasise the just treatment of workers: fair wages, safe conditions, and honest dealings. Investments should therefore support companies that uphold labour dignity and avoid those that exploit employees or rely on unjust labour practices. Jewish tradition also cautions against reckless speculation. The duty to protect one's family means investing with prudence, avoiding excessive risk, and steering clear of get-rich-quick schemes. This perspective reinforces modern advice to prioritise long-term, stable, value-aligned investments.

- Additionally, Judaism views wealth not merely as a private resource but as something entrusted to us for the benefit of the wider community. Ethical investing inspired by this outlook supports businesses that uplift society, create jobs, and contribute to communal well-being.

- Jewish law places strong emphasis on honesty in business, including fair measurement, truthful representation, and transparency. Ethical investors can draw on this by preferring companies with strong governance standards, integrity, and clean compliance records.

3.4 Conclusion

In this chapter, we have discussed some of the ethical guidelines about money and investing, which we can learn from Jewish wisdom. We can leverage some of these principles when deciding where to invest our money.

References

https://thejewishnews.com/2020/09/09/a-jewish-approach-to-planning-and-investing/

https://aish.com/jewish_view_of_money/

Chapter 4: Guidelines for ethical investing from religions: Christianity

In this chapter, we discuss some guidelines for ethical investing taken from Christianity, in particular Catholicism, which we can leverage in building an ethical approach to investing.

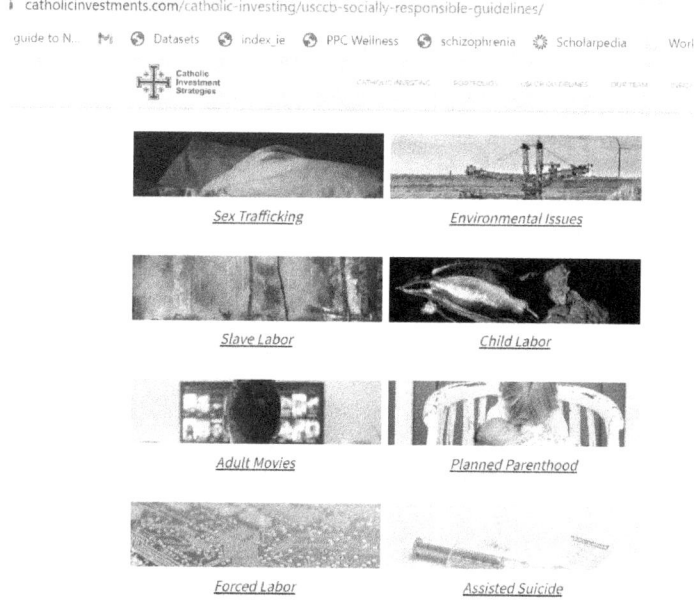

Figure: Screenshot of a website discussing catholic investment strategies for ethical investing

4.1 Catholic guidelines

Catholic guidelines for ethical investing include the following:

- Avoid evil, meaning do not invest in places that promote morally questionable actions such as pornography, racial and gender discrimination, arms production, stem cell research, abortion, slave labor, child labor, predatory lending and so on.

- Do good, meaning to invest in places that work towards protecting human life and dignity, economic justice, environment and encourage corporate responsibility. Also, be active shareholders and take an interest in the policies of the companies where you invest, attend and vote in the shareholder meetings and actively work to improving the company policies.

4.2 Other principles we can learn from Christianity

A central idea in Christian finance is stewardship, the belief that wealth ultimately belongs to God, and people are merely caretakers. This encourages responsible use of money, avoiding greed, and directing resources toward activities that support human dignity and the common good.

Christian Social Teaching highlights a "preferential option for the poor," meaning that financial choices should avoid harming vulnerable communities and ideally support their well-being. Ethical investors inspired by Christianity therefore favour companies that uplift workers, promote fair wages, and avoid exploitative practices.

Biblical teachings repeatedly stress honesty in business, including fair dealings, transparency, and truthfulness. Ethical investors following Christian principles naturally avoid companies engaged in corruption, fraud, or deceptive business practices.

Christian social thought warns strongly against usury and exploitative lending practices. In modern investing, this translates into avoiding companies involved in predatory loans, abusive financial products, and schemes that trap people in debt.

Many contemporary Christian financial teachers suggest that money choices are part of one's moral life. Investing is seen as an extension of Christian values, such as supporting companies that promote dignity, fairness, and care for the community.

Christian-inspired investment groups increasingly practice shareholder activism, using their ownership rights to encourage companies toward ethical policies on the environment, worker rights, and human dignity. This aligns with the Christian commitment to justice and accountability.

References:
https://www.catholicinvestments.com/catholic-investing/usccb-socially-responsible-guidelines/

https://www.faithinvest.org/christianity-finance

Chapter 5: Guidelines for ethical investing from religions: Islam

In this chapter, we discuss some guidelines for ethical investing taken from Islamic principles.

5.1 Islamic guidelines from the Holy Quran

The Holy Quran prohibits interest or **Riba**, views riba as an exploitative and unjust practice that harms individuals and society. It also encourages believers to donate money to needy people as Zaqat.

Quran in chapter 2, verse 275, states:

"Those who consume interest cannot stand [on the Day of Resurrection] except as one stands who is being beaten by Satan into insanity. That is because they say, "Trade is [just] like interest." But Allah has permitted trade and has forbidden interest. So whoever has received an admonition from his Lord and desists may have what is past, and his affair rests with Allah. But whoever returns to [dealing in interest or usury] - those are the companions of the Fire; they will abide eternally therein."

Hence, for Shariah compliant investing, companies and funds should not be getting most of their income from interest, rather than from the proceeds of honest business.

The Quran Chapter 30, verse 39 states:

"And whatever you give for interest to increase within the wealth of people will not increase with Allah. But what you give in zakah (charity), desiring the countenance of Allah - those are the multipliers."

5.2 How Islamic finance treats money

Islamic finance treats money purely as a medium of exchange rather than a commodity to be traded for guaranteed gain. This principle discourages speculative investing and encourages financing linked to real assets and shared economic activity, reinforcing the broader ethical-investing goal of reducing financial harm caused by excessive speculation.

In Islamic finance, two partnership models offer useful ethical ideas. *Musharaka* is a joint partnership where all partners put in money and share profits according to an agreed ratio, while losses are shared in proportion to how much each person invested. Everyone has a stake in the success of the venture, which encourages fairness, honesty, and shared responsibility.

Mudaraba is a different kind of partnership: one person provides the capital and the other provides the skill and labour. Profits are shared, but if a genuine business loss occurs, it is borne by the investor alone unless the manager has acted carelessly or dishonestly. The manager's "loss" is simply not receiving any income for their effort. This structure highlights trust, accountability, and the idea that financial gain should come from real work rather than guaranteed returns.

Together, these two models show how Islamic finance encourages fair risk-sharing and avoids exploitation, principles that fit naturally within an ethical investing framework. Ethical investing frameworks can draw from this when evaluating whether a company distributes risk fairly or merely externalises it.

5.3 Guidelines for Shariah compliant investing

Some shariah financial principles include the following:

- **Ijarah**, meaning leasing an asset to another party for an agreed rental payment over a specified period. It is Shariah-compliant because returns are earned from the use of a tangible asset, not from interest.

- **Sukuk Bond** which is an Islamic bond that can generate returns to investors without being involved with Riba or interest.

One important guideline for Islamic investments is that the funds invested are deployed in carefully managed finance schemes and the profit earned is very close to the market rather than generated from speculation.

It also involves avoiding investing in companies that make their money from the sale of alcohol, abusive drugs, pork products, gambling, weapons, and other such products.

A key Shariah principle is that financial returns should not be guaranteed without sharing the underlying risk. This perspective enriches the ethical-investing critique of predatory lending and encourages investors to favour transparent, risk-aligned business models.

Shariah-compliant finance favours asset-backed investments, such as infrastructure, real goods, and productive enterprises, over purely financial speculation. This overlaps with modern ethical investing, which increasingly favours real-economy sectors such as renewable energy, affordable housing, and sustainable agriculture.

Islamic ethical screens extend beyond product categories to include business conduct. Activities involving deception, unlawful seizure, or unfair advantage are categorically excluded. This can be used to strengthen ethical-investing screens for corporate governance and fair-trade practices.

5.4 Conclusion

In this chapter we have briefly reviewed some Islamic guidelines for money management and investing.

References:

https://taqwabanking.com/faqs.php

https://www.faithinvest.org/islam-and-finance

Dr. Mohamed Saeed Shingeri. A practical model of Islamic Banking, 3rd Edition.

Chapter 6: Guidelines for ethical investing from religions: Buddhism

In this chapter, we discuss some guidelines for ethical investing taken from Buddhism.

6.1 General principles about money from Buddhist texts

The Buddha taught that attachment to wealth is a source of suffering. Generosity (dāna) is one of the "perfections." The ideal is neither poverty nor greed, but right relationship to money—using it skilfully and with compassion.

- "Just as a bee takes nectar without harming the flower, so should a wise person use wealth." (Dhammapada)

6.2 Buddhist guidelines from Sigalovada sutta

According to the Buddha's teachings in Sigalovada sutta and other suttas, one needs to keep the following points in mind:

- One should be mindful of one's money, since it is a type of energy which can be both good or bad.

- Save aside money for times of need as well as invest in growing your business and career.

- Avoid vices that dissipate your wealth such as gambling and excessive greed

- Avoid cheating and lying and follow the precepts and moderation

- Do not be too attached to anything including money and profits.

6.3 Buddhist ethical principles

Buddhist teachers often emphasize the principle of enough or contentment. Financial anxiety often comes from confusing needs with limitless wants. Buddhism teaches that nothing exists independently, rather every choice affects many others. Applied to money, this means that our investments are not isolated transactions but part of a wider web of impact. Additionally, Buddhist psychology describes mental habits such as craving, fear, and avoidance. These show up clearly in financial behavior, including panic-selling during market dips, overconfidence during booms, or ignoring financial responsibilities. Also, Buddhism teaches impermanence (anicca). Markets rise and fall in the same way emotions come and go. Recognizing this reduces fear during downturns and over-excitement during bubbles.

Compassion (karuṇa) is central to Buddhist ethics. Applied to investing, compassion means evaluating not just financial return but whether the investment causes harm or supports well-being. This aligns naturally with ethical investing, preferring companies that treat workers fairly, reduce environmental harm, and contribute positively to society. Similarly, Right Livelihood, one of the steps of Buddha's 8-fold noble path, traditionally refers to earning money without causing harm.

A Buddhist-inspired investing approach points out that knowing your personal "enough" prevents greed-driven decisions and encourages slower, value-aligned investment choices. A simple practice recommended by Buddhist-influenced financial planners (Abacus Wealth Management) is the "Mindful Pause", which means pausing and taking a few breaths before buying or selling an investment. This slows impulsive decisions and allows investors to ask: Does this choice align with my values? Even a short pause creates space for wiser and more ethical decisions.

In the book "Its not about the money" by Brent Kessel, founder of Abacus Wealth Partners, which advocates application of Buddhist ethical principles for wealth management, the author advocates a few principles and practices as follows:

- Being mindful to the stories we make about money, based on our background and experiences and how we were raised. This also involves knowing our money personality or financial archetype, such as pleasure seeker, saver, idealist etc.

- Cultivating equanimity with money, by stopping from reacting to every thought immediately.

- Being stoic about short term losses and not too greedy about getting rich quick strategies. Practicing to let go.

- Practicing the money breath, which involves counting mindfully from 1 to 10 while breathing slowly and mindfully in and out when facing any money problem and being aware of one's thoughts and sensations in the moment.

- Cultivating practices such as giving to good causes and with the right motivation

- Being conscious about the impact we are making with our money and where we are investing.

6.4 Conclusion

In this chapter we have discussed some practices for investing and managing one's money taken from Buddhism.

References:

https://buddhaweekly.com/the-secular-buddhist-approach-to-managing-money-wisely-as-taught-in-sutra/

https://abacuswealth.com/why-buddhism-financial-planning-and-investing-belong-together/

Chapter 7: Guidelines for ethical investing from religions: Hinduism

In this chapter, we discuss some guidelines for ethical investing taken from Hinduism.

7.1 General principles on money from Hinduism

The goddess Lakshmi personifies abundance, but the pursuit of artha (material prosperity) must be balanced with dharma (righteousness), kama (pleasure), and moksha (liberation).

In many Hindu teachings, wealth isn't just a private reward, rather it is a responsibility. It's associated with Lakshmi (the goddess of wealth and prosperity), but prosperity is to be balanced with Seva (selfless service) and duty to community. Therefore, wealth must be treated as a trust, something granted, not just earned, and should be used responsibly. This encourages investors to think not only about personal gain, but about how financial resources can serve larger social good, support community wellbeing, and contribute to meaningful causes rather than purely material accumulation.

Hindu wisdom often teaches moderation: contentment with what one has, combined with voluntary generosity. Investing, accordingly, shouldn't aim solely at maximizing returns; it should also respect balance. A Hindu-inspired ethical investor values generosity and giving: supporting social welfare, philanthropy, and the welfare of others, rather than hoarding or seeking wealth for egoistic ends.

In Hindu philosophy, a key principle is Dharma, the moral order, virtue, and righteous duty. Financial decisions should align with Dharma: fairness, justice, non-harm, honesty.

Hindu tradition's emphasis on Seva reframes investing not only as a personal financial activity but as a potential instrument for positive social change. Ethical investors might deliberately direct capital toward businesses or funds that contribute to health, education, renewable energy, fair labour, effectively combining profit with purpose.

Hindu–philosophical teachings (also echoed in the broader Indian spiritual tradition) encourage detachment: wealth is transient, needs are many, but inner peace matters more than excess. This helps temper greed and fear (fear of loss, anxiety), which often drive poor investing decisions.

7.2 Hinduism guidelines from the Bhagavad Gita

According to the principles in the karma yoga chapter of the Bhagavad Gita, the holy text of Hinduism:

- One should try and become a nishkaama or detached karma yogi, invest well after good research, work hard and honestly and get wealth.

- However, it is also important not to be attached too much to the fruits of one's work and the returns from one's investments.

- In short, do your homework before investing, but keep expectations realistic and do not fall into greed to get high profits.

References:

https://www.speakingtree.in/blog/bhagavad-gita-and-wealth-creation-626486

7.3 Conclusion

In this chapter, we have discussed some of the ethical guidelines about money and investing from Hinduism.

Chapter 8: Guidelines and Insights from Greek and Western Philosophy on Money

Throughout history, philosophers have grappled with the meaning of money, its impact on society, and how best to use it for a good life. Just as world religions offer guidance for ethical investing, so too do the great thinkers of Greece and the Western world. Their teachings highlight that money, while necessary, must always serve higher values—such as virtue, justice, and community.

8.1 Aristotle's View: Money as a Means, Not an End

Aristotle (384–322 BCE), one of the most influential philosophers in history, wrote extensively about money in his works *Nicomachean Ethics* and *Politics*. Aristotle saw money as a practical tool invented to facilitate exchange and meet the genuine needs of people.

- Natural and Unnatural Wealth: Aristotle made an important distinction between using money for natural needs (food, shelter, well-being) and using it purely to accumulate more wealth. He cautioned against turning the pursuit of money into life's main goal, warning that this "unnatural" use leads to greed and social harm.

"Wealth is evidently not the good we are seeking; for it is merely useful and for the sake of something else." — *Nicomachean Ethics*, I.5

- Practical Application: Ethical investors can learn from Aristotle by focusing on investments that support genuine human well-being—not just endless profit.

8.2 The Stoic Approach: Inner Wealth and Contentment

The Stoic philosophers, including Seneca, Epictetus, and Marcus Aurelius, believed that external wealth is neither good nor bad in itself; what matters is our attitude toward it.

- Self-Control Over Desires: The Stoics taught that happiness comes from mastering one's desires, practicing moderation, and being content with "enough." Money is best used as a tool for virtue and service, not status or excessive consumption.

"Wealth consists not in having great possessions, but in having few wants." — Seneca, *Letters from a Stoic*

- Generosity and Detachment: The Stoics recommended using surplus wealth to help others and not becoming emotionally attached to possessions, as fortune can always change.

- Practical   Application: Modern investors can apply Stoic wisdom by avoiding envy and anxiety about market fluctuations, practicing gratitude, and focusing on long-term goals.

8.3 Plato's Warning: Money, Virtue, and Social Harmony

Plato (427–347 BCE), Aristotle's teacher, explored the role of money in society in his famous work *The Republic*.

- Virtue   Above   Wealth: Plato argued that true happiness and a harmonious society are only possible when virtue is valued above material wealth. Pursuing money at all costs can lead to injustice and division.

- Social   Responsibility: For Plato, wealth should be used to build a just and equitable society, not to create divisions or exploit the vulnerable.

8.4 Later Western Philosophers: Ethics, Society, and the Role of Money

a) Thomas Aquinas and Medieval Thought

- Means to an End: Medieval philosophers like Thomas Aquinas, drawing on Aristotle and Christian values, emphasized that money should only be a means to support family, community, and acts of charity. Greed (*avaritia*) was considered a moral failing.

b) Adam Smith: Markets with Morality

- Sympathy and Justice: Adam Smith, known as the father of modern economics, believed that while markets can promote prosperity, they require trust, fairness, and moral restraint to function well. In *The Theory of Moral Sentiments*, Smith stressed empathy and justice as necessary companions to economic activity.

c) Karl Marx: Alienation and Social Impact

- Warning Against Exploitation: Karl Marx critiqued the way money, under unchecked capitalism, can alienate people from their work and each other. He warned against letting profit motives override human needs and social good.

d) Max Weber: Values and the Spirit of Capitalism

- Ethics   Shape   Economics:
  Max Weber explored how Western religious and
  cultural values—like hard work, honesty, and
  delayed gratification—influenced the rise of
  modern capitalism. He cautioned that losing sight
  of these values could lead to a soulless, purely
  mechanical economic system.

8.5   Modern   Western   Thought: Behavioural Economics and Money Mindset

Recent Western thinkers have increasingly turned their attention to the psychology of money:

- Behavioural   Economics:
  Scholars such as Daniel Kahneman and Richard
  Thaler have shown that people are often irrational
  about money, prone to biases like loss aversion
  and short-term thinking. Awareness of these
  tendencies helps investors make wiser, less
  emotional choices.

- Wealth   and   Happiness:
  Modern   writers   like   Morgan   Housel   (*The
  Psychology of Money*) emphasize that true wealth
  is not just financial, but also emotional—a sense of
  security, freedom, and enough-ness.

8.6 Lessons for Ethical Investors

Drawing from Greek and Western philosophy, several principles stand out for anyone wishing to invest ethically and mindfully:

- Let Money Serve You, Not Rule You: Use money as a tool to achieve meaningful goals, not as life's main purpose.

- Moderation and Contentment: Practice self-restraint and recognize what is "enough" for you.

- Generosity and Justice: Share your surplus, invest in causes that promote social good, and avoid investments that exploit or harm others.

- Long-Term Perspective: Focus on patient, values-driven investing, not short-term speculation or fads.

- Self-Knowledge and Reflection: Regularly examine your beliefs and habits about money, aiming for wisdom over mere accumulation.

8.7 Conclusion

Greek and Western philosophers remind us that money is powerful, but its value depends on how we use it. Ethical investing, in this tradition, is not just about what we buy or avoid, but about the mindset and virtues we cultivate—gratitude, moderation, fairness, and service to others. By integrating these timeless lessons, investors can build both material and moral wealth.

References

- Aristotle, *Nicomachean Ethics*, *Politics*

- Plato, *The Republic*

- Seneca, *Letters from a Stoic*

- Adam Smith, *The Theory of Moral Sentiments*, *The Wealth of Nations*

- Karl Marx, *Capital*

- Max Weber, *The Protestant Ethic and the Spirit of Capitalism*

- Morgan Housel, *The Psychology of Money*

- Daniel Kahneman, *Thinking, Fast and Slow*

- Richard Thaler & Cass Sunstein, *Nudge*

Chapter 9: Some books about the psychology of money

Understanding financial psychology is crucial for making rational investment decisions. This chapter reviews books that explore behavioral finance, emotional influences on money management, and the mindset needed for successful investing. This is relevant since if we handle money with a certain commonsense and a good psychology, we would be more likely to have a good relationship with money and be in a chance to make more money.

9.1 Happy money: the Japanese art of making peace with your money by Ken Honda

happy money

The Japanese Art of Making Peace with Your Money

ken honda
JAPAN'S BESTSELLING ZEN MILLIONAIRE

Author website: https://kenhonda.com/

Amazon link https://www.amazon.com/Happy-Money-Japanese-Making-Peace/dp/1501188372

In this book, Ken Honda offers what he calls a Zen-like approach to money, a philosophy learned in large part from his mentor, the legendary Japanese investor Wahei Takeda, sometimes dubbed "the Warren Buffett of Japan." Honda's core message is that money is not merely a neutral medium of exchange; it is charged with the emotional energy we attach to it. We can choose to create a relationship with money that is joyful and life-affirming rather than anxious or adversarial.

Money as Living Energy

Honda teaches that money behaves like a living current. It carries the emotional imprint of the way it is earned and spent. "Happy Money" is money that arrives or departs with gratitude, generosity and trust; "Unhappy Money" is burdened with fear, resentment or guilt. The difference is not in the denomination but in the energy that accompanies each transaction.

The Practice of "Arigato Money"

Central to Honda's teaching is the simple but powerful practice of saying "arigato" (thank you) to money both when it comes in and when it goes out. When you receive your salary or a small gift, silently thank the money. When you pay a bill or donate to a cause, thank the money again for the service it provides and the connections it represents. This ritual transforms routine financial acts into moments of mindfulness and gratitude, breaking the cycle of worry that often surrounds money.

"Maro-Up": Cultivating Inner Qualities

Honda introduces the term "Maro-Up," drawn from an old Japanese word for a pure, sincere heart. To "maro-up" is to consciously cultivate kindness, generosity, gratitude, mindfulness and appreciation. Wahei believed that these qualities create an atmosphere in which wealth—financial and otherwise—naturally multiplies. An abundance mentality does not mean reckless spending; it means trusting that there is enough and that sharing strengthens, rather than weakens, your own security.

Healing Money Wounds

Many people carry "money wounds", which are fears and limiting beliefs learned in childhood or absorbed from cultural narratives about scarcity, status or shame. Honda encourages bringing these patterns to light and forgiving oneself and one's family for past mistakes. Awareness and compassion loosen the grip of these inherited anxieties and free us to relate to money with curiosity and calm.

Abundance versus Scarcity

Both Honda and Wahei argue that abundance is primarily a mindset. Scarcity thinking treats every payment as a loss and hoards wealth in fear of the future. Abundance thinking recognises that the world contains enough resources for all and that generosity often attracts unexpected opportunities. Modern behavioural research supports this: people who trust in "enough" experience lower stress and make more patient financial decisions.

The core principles of Happy Money are as follows:

- Money is Energy. Each rupee or yen carries the emotional signature of how it is earned and used.

- Gratitude. Every transaction can be an act of thanks.

- Flow and Circulation. Money, like water, stagnates when hoarded and nourishes when it moves.

- Healing Money Wounds. Acknowledge and forgive the past to create freedom in the present.

- Abundance over Scarcity. Trust that sharing strengthens wealth rather than depletes it.

"If you treat money with love and respect, it will smile back at you." – Ken Honda, *Happy Money* (2019)

Honda often summarises his mentor's teachings in five disciplines:

1. Smile first – Approach business and life with open friendliness; trust attracts cooperation.

2. Give first – Offer value or help before expecting a reward.

3. Praise first – Recognise others' contributions, which strengthens networks of goodwill.

4. Empathise first – Understand the needs and feelings of those you deal with; money follows meaningful relationships.

5. Thank first – Gratitude, expressed often and sincerely, keeps the flow of money and goodwill alive.

Practical Tools for Daily Life

- Thank your money. Whisper or think "arigato" each time you receive or spend, turning finance into a daily gratitude practice.

- Notice emotional imprints. Ask whether the money you earn and spend carries joy or resentment, and adjust how you earn or give accordingly.

- Give freely within your means. A small, regular gift—to a neighbour, a charity, or someone in need—keeps the flow alive.

- Automate generosity. As Wahei did, consider setting aside a fixed percentage of income for giving; automation turns intention into habit.

- Heal old narratives. Reflect on family stories about money, forgive past mistakes, and consciously write a new one based on trust and gratitude.

- Visualise the benefit. Wahei recommended picturing the people who will be helped by your future wealth—your children, your community, or even a stranger who benefits from your charitable bequest.

Honda and Wahei ultimately invite us to see money as a mirror of character. By cultivating gratitude, generosity and mindfulness, we not only reduce financial anxiety but also attract opportunities and relationships that reinforce abundance. In this view, making peace with money is not simply a financial skill; it is a path to a more spacious, meaningful life.

9.2 Work, Sex, Money: Real Life on the Path of Mindfulness by Chogyam Trungpa

Amazon link https://www.amazon.com/Work-Sex-Money-Real-Mindfulness-ebook/dp/B00HZ374DG

Seminar link where the author gave teachings of the book https://www.chronicleproject.com/work-sex-money-seminar-three/

This book is by the famous Tibetan Buddhist meditation teacher Chogyam Trungpa, based on the teachings he gave to his students in the west. In this book, he covers how we can have a mindful and genuine approach to money. We should not be attached or be obsessed with money, but cultivate a spirit of generosity and giving. Money is a kind of energy. Its neither good nor bad, but depends on our attitude to it. Handling money well is a part of our spiritual practice. We should manage our finances in such a way as to cultivate a balanced life, with mindful earning, spending and consumption of money.

9.3 Mind over money: Why understanding your money behaviour will improve your financial freedom by Evan Lucas

MIND

OVER

M $ NEY

Why understanding your money behaviour
will improve your financial freedom

EVAN LUCAS

Author website https://www.evan-lucas.com/book

Amazon link https://www.amazon.com/Mind-over-Money-understanding-behaviour/dp/1922611484

In this book, the author Evan Lucas delves into the psychology of money and why people behave the way they do about money. The author urges the reader to reflect on what money really means to them, what are the personal experiences they had with money and what drives their behavior and attitudes towards money.

The book discusses a few kinds of short-term and long-term behavioral biases that affect the way people deal with money, such as an aversion to risk, attitude to delayed returns and discounts, loss aversion, availability bias, anchoring, cutting corners, confirmation bias, herd mentality, short-term greed and so on, and how these are affected by culture, illustrating the concepts with various examples. It advises the reader to identify their and their partner's money personality: spender or saver or investor or one who ignores it. Finally, it urges the reader to keep track of one's finances, budgeting, discusses loans and insurance, and gives an overview of different asset classes such as property and shares and how to have realistic expectations of each.

9.4 The Psychology of Money: Timeless lessons on wealth, greed, and happiness by Morgan Housel

Amazon link: https://www.amazon.com/Psychology-Money-Timeless-lessons-happiness/dp/0857197681

Author website https://www.morganhousel.com/

In this book, the author goes through different aspects of the psychology of money. The book points out that financial success is not about what knowledge we have of money, but how we put it into practice, and at times of crisis such as financial crashes we will know our actual behavior. It emphasizes long term thinking and patience which are essential to grow our money, and discusses the power of compounding and the role of time. Saving money is essential to deal with uncertainties in life. Some people will always have more money than us, so it is important to know when to be satisfied. Different people have different levels of tolerance to risk, and we are often influenced by emotions when making financial decisions. We often like to tell ourselves stories about money, partly influenced by our past, that governs our behaviours.

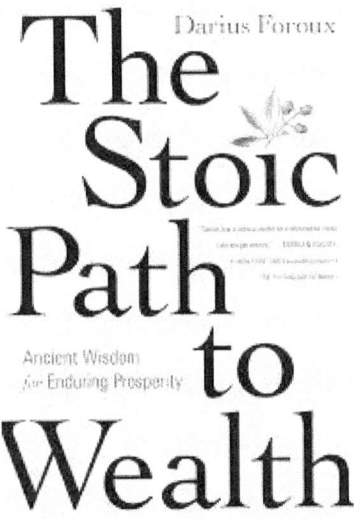

9.5 The Stoic Path to Wealth by Darius Foroux

Amazon link: https://www.amazon.com/Stoic-Path-Wealth-Enduring-Prosperity/dp/0593544153/

Author website: https://dariusforoux.com/stoic-path-to-wealth/

This book advocates an approach to wealth with ideas from stoic philosophy, including: managing one's emotions and being level-headed, especially when dealing with loss, pragmatically managing risk, growing wealth while living with values such as integrity, ignoring short-term fluctuations in one's portfolio and having a long-term mindset that can control greed. Stoic philosophy can help the investor to maintain a cool mind through adversity and losses.

9.6 Mind Over Money: Overcoming the Money Disorders That Threaten Our Financial Health by Brad Klontz and Ted Klontz

Amazon link: https://www.amazon.com/Mind-Over-Money-Overcoming-Disorders/dp/0385530846

Author   website:
https://www.yourmentalwealthadvisors.com/
This book explores the concept of "money scripts"—the
unconscious beliefs we develop about money from
childhood, family, and culture. The Klontz duo, both
psychologists, explain how these deep-rooted beliefs
influence our earning, saving, spending, and investing
behaviors. The book provides practical exercises to
identify and rewrite your own money scripts, helping
readers heal from financial anxiety, scarcity thinking, and
self-sabotage.
Key lessons from the book include: Recognize and
challenge unhealthy money beliefs; develop healthier
money habits for lasting well-being.

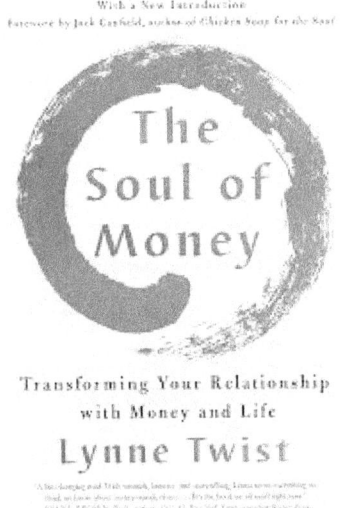

9.7 The Soul of Money: Transforming Your Relationship with Money and Life by Lynne Twist

Amazon link: https://www.amazon.com/Soul-Money-Transforming-Relationship/dp/039332950X

Author website: https://soulofmoney.org/ Lynne Twist draws on decades of philanthropic experience to show how money can become a force for personal transformation and positive social change. She examines the "myth of scarcity" and encourages an "enough" mindset—living and investing in ways that align with your values, purpose, and gratitude. Key lessons from the book include: Move from fear and scarcity to sufficiency and generosity; use money as a tool for a meaningful, purpose-driven life.

9.8 Nudge: Improving Decisions About Health, Wealth, and Happiness by Richard Thaler and Cass Sunstein

Amazon link: https://www.amazon.com/Nudge-Improving-Decisions-Health-Happiness/dp/014311526X
Author websites: https://www.richardthaler.com/ and https://cas.sunstein.org/

A foundational text in behavioral economics, this book explains how simple "nudges" in our environment—such as automating savings or setting better defaults—can help us overcome biases and improve financial decisions. Nudge offers practical techniques to design better financial habits and systems for yourself and your community.

Key lessons from the book include: Use "choice architecture" to make saving, investing, and giving easier and more consistent; overcome inertia and emotional traps.

9.9 Your Money or Your Life by Vicki Robin and Joe Dominguez

Amazon link: https://www.amazon.com/Your-Money-Life-Transforming-Relationship/dp/0143115766

Author website: https://yourmoneyoryourlife.com/

This classic guide redefines money—not just as a means to buy things, but as "life energy." The book offers a nine-step program to transform your relationship with money, track your spending, build financial independence, and focus on what truly brings satisfaction.

Key lessons from the book include: Discover your "enough"; align money management with your deepest values and long-term happiness.

9.10 The Art of Money: A Life-Changing Guide to Financial Happiness by Bari Tessler

Amazon link: https://www.amazon.com/Art-Money-Life-Changing-Financial-Happiness/dp/1946764102

Author website: https://baritessler.com/

Blending practical advice with mindfulness and self-reflection, Bari Tessler's book introduces "financial therapy"—the practice of bringing emotional intelligence and awareness to money decisions. She helps readers gently examine money fears, cultivate gratitude, and develop clear, compassionate money practices for every stage of life.

Key lessons: Heal old money wounds; integrate emotions, values, and practical tools for a balanced approach to wealth.

9.11 The Little Book of Behavioral Investing: How Not to Be Your Own Worst Enemy by James Montier

Amazon link: https://www.amazon.com/Little-Book-Behavioral-Investing-Profitable/dp/0470686022

James Montier, a renowned behavioral economist, offers a practical and research-backed guide to avoiding the most common psychological mistakes in investing—such as overconfidence, loss aversion, herding, and recency bias.

Key lessons from the book include: Learn to recognize and manage your own biases to make smarter investment decisions.

9.12 Conclusion

Psychological factors play a critical role in investing. By understanding biases and adopting a mindful approach, investors can make better financial decisions. The next chapter will focus on general investment principles applicable to ethical investing.

Chapter 10: General investing principles

Before diving into ethical investing, it is essential to understand basic investment principles. This chapter covers risk assessment, diversification, and long-term strategies for building a sustainable investment portfolio.

10.1 Basic steps before one starts investing

A good investor should first be mindful of their monthly income and expenses, and what is their net worth. It is useful to work this out in a spreadsheet if one has not done so already.

Once this is done, every month one should aim to first pay off as early as possible their high interest debts like credit cards and personal loans, since the interest is highest in these.

After that, one should have at least the following, by checking if one has these already and if not, making the effort to build them up:

- Emergency fund: This means a few months' worth of savings in a fixed deposit or FDs for unforeseen emergencies.

- Put aside at least 10-20% of their disposable income each month in investing, whether in stocks, mutual funds, bonds, gold or other asset classes.

- Put aside some percentage of their salary each month towards safe retirement options such as Provident Funds (EPF and PPF) and Pension Schemes such as National Pension Scheme (NPS).

- Have a good term insurance and health insurance policy at a minimum.

It is a good principle to put aside money for investment each month upon getting one's salary before paying for one's regular expenses like groceries and transport. The earlier one starts investing, the better returns one can get, since the money has more time to grow, because of the power of compounding.

10.2 Analyzing one's risk profile

One should do an analysis of their risk profile to know what kind of investor they are. This can partly depend on one's background and partly on factors such as their age, money already saved, time remaining till retirement, number of dependents, long term debts one has and other factors.

According to the risk profile, one can be one of the following types: cautious, balanced or aggressive.

Accordingly, below is the strategy to invest as per the risk profile:

- **Cautious investor**: Keep more percentage of bonds and less of stocks in their portfolio.

- **Balanced investor**: Keep a good mix of stocks and bonds and gold as per your age.

- **Aggressive investor**: Mostly stocks and very less bonds.

It is never a good idea to put all one's financial eggs in the same basket, since the market can fall or rise suddenly depending on the conditions. Therefore, the investing should be in a mixture of different classes: stocks, bonds, gold, real estate, mutual funds and crypto and riskier assets.

One should also decide on how much to invest in different asset classes, as per their risk profile and age. The older one is and closer to retirement, the more they should invest in less risky options such as bonds and less in stocks. Therefore, when one is younger, one may decide to invest more into stocks and equity based mutual funds, while as one gets older one can go for a mix of stocks, bonds, equity and debt mutual funds, gold and other assets.

One should be very aware of the power of compounding and the fact that time is the most important asset. Accordingly, the earlier one starts to invest money, the better it is since it has more time to compound. But it is also never too late to start, even if one is already in their late 30s or 40s or even 50s.

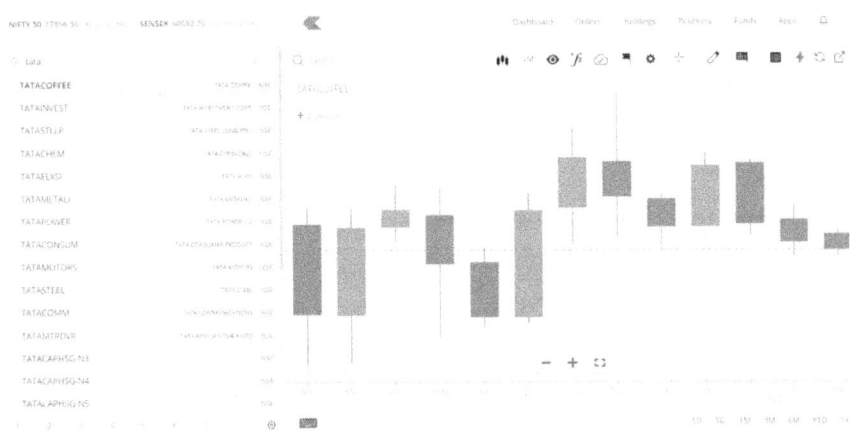

Figure: Screenshot from zerodha kite trading platform

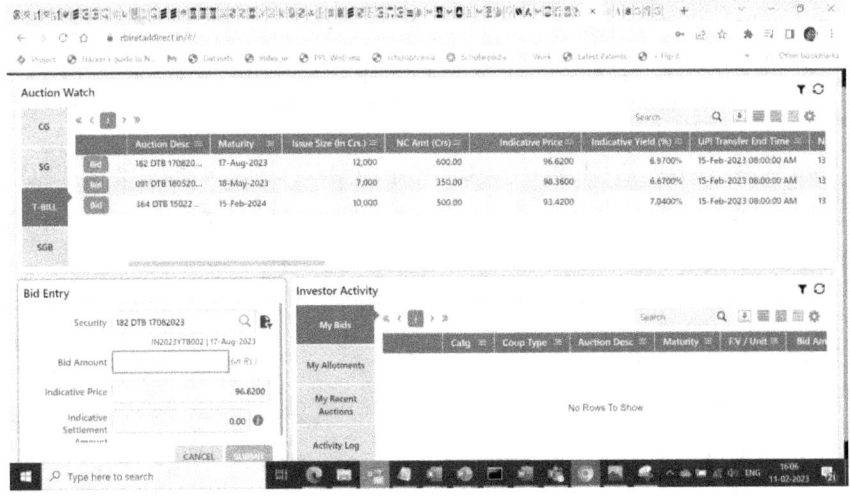

Figure: Screenshot from RBI retail direct website showing T bills

10.3 Investment in stocks

Company shares, or stocks, are the most common way to invest. They usually give good returns from appreciation in the value of the stock, as well as periodic dividends.

To trade in shares, one can have a free account with an Indian stockbroker. Common stockbrokers include Zerodha, 5paisa, Upstox, Angel one, kotak securities, Motilal Oswal, Groww, Sharekhan, Kotak Mahindra, ICICI Direct or any other broker. These may have different fees structures and value-added services, so one needs to carefully check these before enrolling.

Out of these, Indmoney, Vested, Groww, IndiaINX and a few other brokers give the option of investing in US and other foreign stocks as well, either by tying up with US-based trading API providers such as Alpaca Securities or mainstream US brokers such as Interactive Brokers.

10.4 Investing in Mutual funds

Mutual funds are a good way to invest, since they spread the risk from individual stocks. Mutual funds usually have a dedicated fund manager who takes care of your money. Another advantage of mutual funds is that they are well regulated by SEBI, a government agency, and so the risk of fraud is lower.

One can invest any amount into mutual funds, as opposed to stocks in India which have to be purchased in whole numbers. Mutual funds have a huge variety and are available for different kinds of stocks, risk profiles, sectors etc.

There are bond or debt mutual funds, equities or stocks mutual funds, tracker funds, liquid funds and so on. Index fund or tracker funds track the whole Sensex such as NSE and BSE Sensex, or a certain part of the Sensex such as Smallcap 250 Index fund. Index funds typically have a lower expense ratio and no exit load. NIFTY-50 and BSE Sensex are some of the main index funds based on the Indian stock markets. To guard against currency fall in value of rupee, one can similarly invest in US based index funds such as Vanguard's VTI, VOO, VT, Invesco's QQQ and so on.

Index funds, or passive funds, are good for lower cost passive investing. Since the stock market usually grows in the long run, it is useful to invest a tracker fund such as NIFTY-50 either as a one time or SIP every month, and watch it grow over time and take advantage of the rising stock market.

Non-index funds, or actively managed funds, on the other hand, may be actively managed and have a higher cost in terms of expense ratio and exit load. But if the fund managers are experienced and from established fund management houses that have been around for a while (such as SBI mutual fund or Parag Parikh mutual fund), good at identifying which stocks to invest and been managing the fund well for the last few years, they may give higher returns.

One should also be careful when buying mutual funds which have made a huge profit very recently but not in earlier years. One should also check the record of the fund manager before deciding to invest, using websites such as Morningstar and Value Research. The best mutual funds are those that have been making consistent profits for at least 4-5 years. Also, they should have a higher amount of AUM or assets under management.

One can invest in mutual funds either by paying a one-time lumpsum, or by doing a SIP where one pays a fixed amount each month to buy the same mutual fund. SIP investing is a better way to guard against fluctuations in the value of the fund.

Mutual funds investment can be of two types: direct and regular. Regular mutual funds charge a little more commission than direct funds, but offered through third parties which may add value with services such as portfolio analysis and rebalancing. New fund offerings or NFOs are when a new mutual fund is launched, sometimes at a discount. Closed mutual funds have a closing date beyond which no new subscriptions are allowed, while open funds have no such restriction.

Mutual funds can be invested via one's stockbroker such as Zerodha coin or Samco RankMF or via dedicated curated mutual funds sites such as Scripbox and FundsIndia.

10.5 Investing in Bonds

Bonds, especially government bonds, are safer but also give lower returns, and are a good hedge against risks from stocks falling in value. One's portfolio should have a mix of stocks and bonds.

On the other hands, since the returns are fixed, bonds may lose money if there is high inflation, the Rupee falls in value compared to US dollar, or when the RBI interest rates rise.

There are two kinds of bonds, government bonds and corporate bonds. Government bonds or treasury bonds are typically the safest but may have lower returns than corporate bonds. When investing in corporate bonds, it is important to check the credit ratings of bonds (such as AAA or AA+). They can be bought from RBI retail direct website or broker sites like zerodha.

10.6 Investing in debt-based government schemes

Other types of debt-based government investing include post office schemes such as **Kisan Vikas Patra** and **National Savings Certificates**, **Senior Citizens Savings Scheme** and **Sukanya Samruddhi Yojana** for daughters. These are all typically safe places to keep your money.

10.7 Investing in Gold

Gold usually is inflation proof, i.e., it does not lose its value during inflation.

One can invest in gold in different forms such as physical gold, digital gold (such as from MMTC PAMP website or apps such as Gullak gold app) and government's Sovereign Gold Bonds.

However, one must beware of taxes such as GST on physical and digital gold, which is not applicable in sovereign gold bonds. Physical gold has other costs such as making charges and cost of bank lockers to store it safely.

10.8 Investing in Real estate

Real estate is another common investment avenue but needs very high amounts of investment, typically 50 lakhs to 1 crore for flats and more for land.

It is better to invest with famous and established builders since their flats will have a better resale value, and in land to invest with municipal authorities in new layouts such as Delhi Development Authority or DDA.

Another low-cost way for property is to invest in Real estate investment trusts (REITs) or fractional ownership of office space. Examples of REITs whose shares can be traded in the Indian stock markets include Embassy REIT and Mindspace REIT.

10.9 Investment in fixed deposits

Another option is to invest in fixed deposits or FDs offered by banks or by private financial companies such as Bajaj Finance.

FDs are usually very safe, have a better interest rate than savings account, but one's money is locked up for the duration of the FD which may be 6 months to a few years. FDs can be offered by one's own bank, such as state bank of India, or by other financial institutions such as Bajaj Capital.

Also, they may have not so high interest rates when compared to inflation, and the interest given is subject to income tax at one's normal tax slab. One may opt for monthly or periodic interest payouts or interest payout at maturity.

Senior citizens typically get better rates in FDs. Recently, many FDs have been giving better rates up to 8.5 or 9% for senior citizens and slightly less for others.

10.10 Investing for one's retirement

It is important to save money in the longer term, for one's retirement.

For retirement, many people have **Employees Provident Fund** or EPF provided by their employers at the place they work, which gives interest of around 8%.

Another option is **Public Provident Fund** or PPF, which is safe and currently gives around 7% interest, which is usually for 15 years but may be extended longer. These investments are beneficial for tax, most of them are claimable tax free under section 80C of the Income Tax.

Another option for retirement is **National Pension Scheme or NPS**, which has two tiers: tier 1 NPS is tax free, but money cannot be withdrawn until one is 60 years of age. ELSS is another tax saving scheme one can use to invest in mutual funds, although one must stay invested for a minimum of 3 years.

10.11 Investing in Insurance schemes

One should also have some form of insurance, to cover unfortunate events such as medical emergencies and death.

These include various forms such as:

- **term insurance** (pays out an amount on death of the policyholder)

- **health insurance** (pays an amount on hospitalization and medical treatments)

- **life insurance** (pay out an amount on death as well as some money on maturity)

Unit Linked Insurance Plans or **ULIPs.**

Out of these, term insurance makes the most sense since it has pure insurance and low premiums. It is best to have insurance in schemes which do not mix insurance and investment.

Here too there is a wide choice of insurance companies such as Life Insurance Corporation of India, ICICI Direct, Tata AIG, HDFC Ergo, Niva Bupa or Max Bupa, Navi etc.

Ditto (by Zerodha) and PolicyBazaar are online insurance advisory platforms that can give unbiased advice on comparing and choosing between different insurance schemes.

10.12 Peer to Peer lending (P2P)

Another investing scheme includes Peer to Peer lending or P2P lending. This is a form of alternative investment in which individuals lend money directly to borrowers through online platforms. Good websites for P2P lending include indiap2p.com (IndiaP2P) and 12% club.

P2P schemes may be relatively safer among most alternative investment schemes.

10.13 Other alternative investments

Other alternative investment schemes include green investments (such as sustvest.com), fractional shares in company property, investing in startups or ESOPs (Employee Stock Option Plans), unlisted shares, movie audio and video rights and so on. However, one should be very careful and do thorough due diligence and research when investing in such alternative schemes and especially in startups.

10.14 PMS or Portfolio Management Services

PMS or **Portfolio Management Services** (sites such as pmsbazaar.com or Dezerv.in) claim to give better returns than mutual funds, but may have higher fees and a higher minimum capital requirement such as minimum investment of 50 lakh rupees.

10.15 Investing in smallcases

Smallcase.com has a number of smallcases such as run by Teji Mandi and Windmill capital, which provide services, where they give suggestions on when to buy and sell some chosen stocks to generate maximum profit, for a fixed fee per year.

10.16 Investing in crypto currencies

Another new way to invest is in **cryptocurrency** such as Bitcoin and Ethereum and Dogecoin and SHIB coin (available in India from platforms such as WazirX and Coinswitch Kuber). Here also one should do due diligence and not take unnecessary risks. One should also remember that crypto gains are currently taxed at a very high rate of 30% in India, with no adjustment for losses.

10.17 Investing in derivatives

More risky and modern ways to invest include **derivatives, forex and commodity trading**. Trading in alternative investments can give faster returns but can also cause bigger losses faster, one should only go for trading if they are willing to invest the time and have the appropriate risk profile and enough training.

10.18 Setting financial goals

One should also think of setting a goal of a corpus to achieve as a result of their investment, such as minimum Rupees 1 to 1.5 crore after 10 to 15 years. Then one should calculate how much to invest every month or every year based on their goal and expected returns. The formula to use is $PV = FV/(1 + i)^n$ where PV = present value, FV = future value, i = interest rate as a decimal (e.g. 0.12 for 12%), and n = number of periods (years). Alternatively, online SIP calculators are available on sites like Groww or Zerodha to make these projections easy.

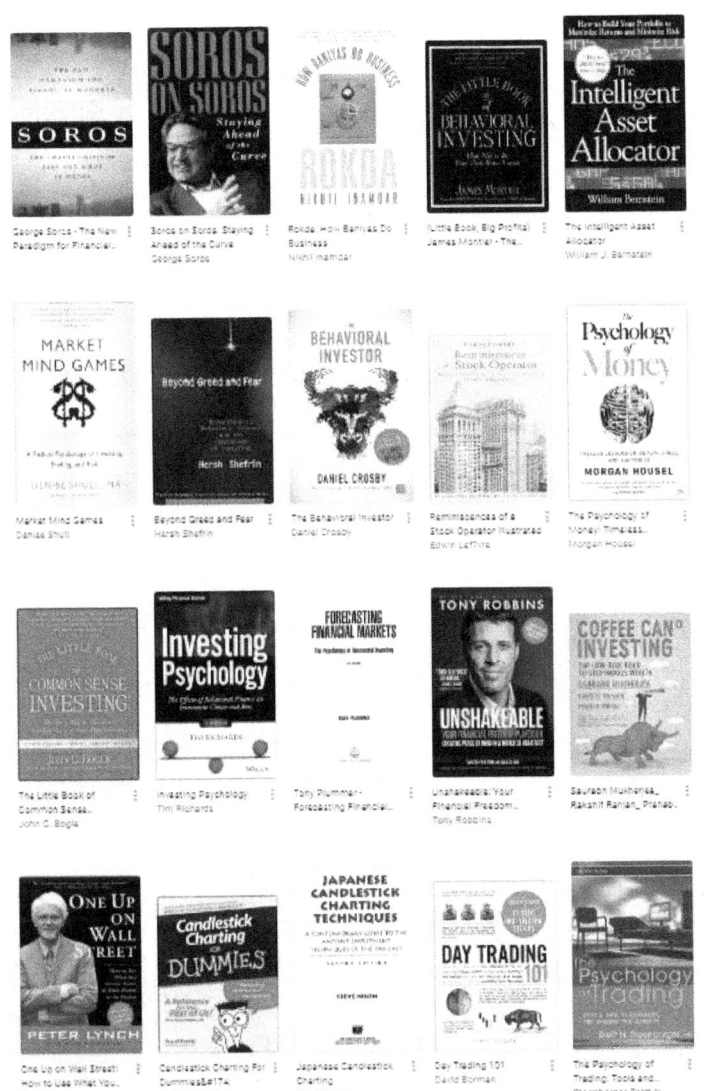

Figure: Screenshot of some good books related to investing and trading

10.19 Books and resources about money management and investing

Some good books about money management include:

- The psychology of money by Morgan Housel

- Money master the game by Tony Robbins

- Rich dad poor dad by Robert Kiyosaki

- Smart Money Moves by Vinod Desai

- The Bee, The Beetle, & the Money Bug – The BankBazaar Guide to the Financial Wild by Adhil Shetty

- All about money by Simon Daniel

- The Little Book of Common Sense Investing by John C. Bogle

Some good books about investing include:

- Let's Talk Money by Monica Halan

- The intelligent investor by Benjamin Graham

- Stocks to Riches by Parag Parikh

- Fundamental analysis for investors by Raghu Palat

- How To Make Money in Stock Market by Rakesh Jhunjhunwala

- Investing 101 by Michele Cagan

- The little book that beats the market by Joel Greenblatt

- The little book of behavioral investing by James Montier

- The intelligent asset allocator by William Bernstein

- Coffee Can Investing by Saurabh Mukherjea and Rakshit Ranjan

- Unshakable by Tony Robbins

- The Motley Fool investment guide by David and Tom Gardner

- One up on Wall Street by Peter Lynch

- The four pillars of investing by William Bernstein

- The Bogleheads guide to investing by John C Bogle

- Investment Advisor (Level 1 and Level 2) by NISM

- The Warren Buffett Way by Robert Hagstrom

- Common Stocks and Uncommon Profits by Philip Fisher

Some books about trading include:

- Technical analysis of the financial markets by John Murphy

- Reminiscences of a stock operator by Edwin Lefevre

- How to make money trading with candlestick charts by Balkrishna Sadekar

- Cashtags by Vishal and Meghana Malkan

It is always better to first learn about investing from books and training courses in YouTube and apps and websites like Investopedia. One should be familiar with the terms by reading financial sections of newspapers and magazines.

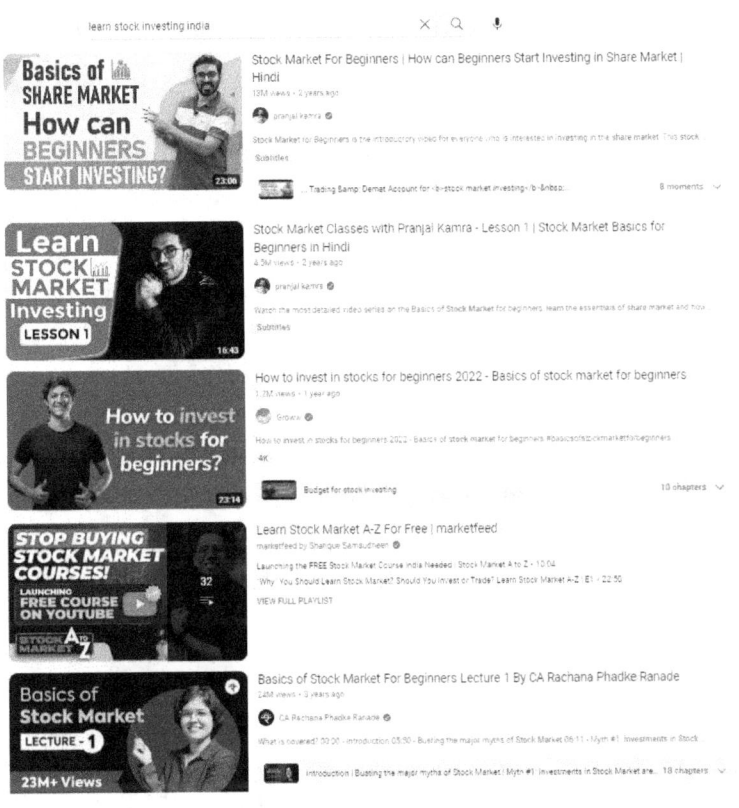

Figure: Screenshot of some YouTube channels to learn stock investing in India

There are a number of good **YouTube channels** related to trading and investing in India. Examples include Sunil Miglani, Trade Brains, Pranjal Kamra, Finnovation Z, Groww, Trading Chanakya, Asset Yogi, Fund Guruji, Learn to Invest, Super Trader Lakshya, Market Maestroo, etc. Some of these may not be suitable for beginners, so one can try an episode and subscribe to those channels which they can understand and are useful.

There are also some good **apps** to learn about the stock market, trading and investments such as Siyona Training academy (good for beginners), investing game, Learn: stock market investing and Cashflow game, Varsity by Zerodha and so on.

Some good **newspapers** include Economic Times, Mint, Hindu Businessline, Financial express, Financial chronicle, Business Standard, Financial times (from UK), Economic Times, Magazines include Outlook money, Capital Market, Dalal Street Investment Journal, Forbes India, Business Today, Businessworld, Business India, the Economist (from UK).

ValueResearch website (www.valueresearch.com), its Youtube channel and its magazines Mutual Funds Insight and Wealth Insight are also good tools where one can read about different aspects of mutual funds and good investing practices, along with rankings and ratings of good mutual funds.

10.20 Some principles to identify good companies to invest

Warren Buffett and Benjamin Graham were advocates of an actively managed stock investing strategy. As per their philosophy, it is better to do proper and thorough research to find the best undervalued stocks that are likely to generate good profits in the long term, rather than the short term.

Some of the important ratios related to fundamental analysis to identify good stocks include the following:

- **Price Per Earnings ratio or P/E ratio**: This is the stock price divided by Earnings per share. This should not be too high relative to other companies in the same sector. A lower PE ratio indicates that the stock represents good value, since its price is not too high compared with the earnings.

- **Dividend Yield**: This is the dividends per share divided by the stock price. A higher dividend yield is better and it should be consistent over the last few years. A good company is one that regularly pays dividends.

- **Debt to Equity ratio or DE ratio** shows how much debt a company has compared to its assets. A lower DE ratio is better.

- **ROI or return on Investment (along with ROCE or return on capital employed)**: These are measures of how profitable the company is, a higher ROI and ROCE is better.

- **Enterprise Value-to-EBITDA (EV/EBITDA) Ratio**: This measures the company's market value relative to its earnings before interest, taxes, depreciation, and amortization. A lower value for this ratio is better.

- **Market cap**: Companies that have a bigger market cap are more likely to be stable and produce regular dividends.

- **Piotroski score**: this is a formula that reflects how much financially strong the company is, a score of at least 7 or 8 or above is better.

One can compare these ratios for different companies to see which one is better. Also, one can put the formula for these ratios in screener.in (or readymade screeners in tickertape.in) to get a list of companies that match the criteria. After that one can read up and do additional research on the companies. It is good to also read up about the company and sector, the general news and specific recent news about the management, understand the unique selling point or USP of the company relative to its competitors.

After one has identified a company to invest using fundamental analysis, one can then use technical analysis to understand the best time to invest in it. Technical analysis involves reading the historical graph of the share price going up or down within last few days or months, and identifying patterns based on its price movements such as candlesticks. Technical analysis techniques are used heavily by day traders to identify when to buy and when to sell a stock.

However, it is better to spend good time in identifying the best stocks and buy a stock for the long term, at least a few years, rather than short term.

10.21 Monitoring one's portfolio

One should also do a periodic review of their investments from time to time and be ready to sell at the right time. Websites like MoneyControl (www.moneycontrol.com) are good for stock analysis and ESG ratings. Google finance (https://www.google.com/finance/?hl=en) is also a good tool to regularly track the performance of one's portfolio.

10.22 Conclusion

In this chapter we have gone through some basic principles of investing in India. Beginners to investing should make a good effort to gain as much knowledge as possible for a few months from different books and other sources before seriously starting to invest. Having a mentor to help with good investing advice is also a useful idea. Applying sound investment principles ensures that ethical investing is both responsible and financially rewarding. In the next chapter, we will discuss how to identify ethical investment opportunities.

Chapter 11: How to search for ethical investing opportunities

Finding ethical investments requires thorough research. This chapter provides a guide to identifying ethical stocks, funds, and investment platforms in India.

11.1 Places to search for ethical funds and stocks

Ethical companies and funds can be searched in the following places (India-specific):

- Money and investing websites such as moneycontrol, cleartax or yahoo finance

- Search engines such as Google or Bing or ChatGPT

- Broker websites such as zerodha, indmoney, sharekhan, 5paisa, upstoxx, icici direct or groww

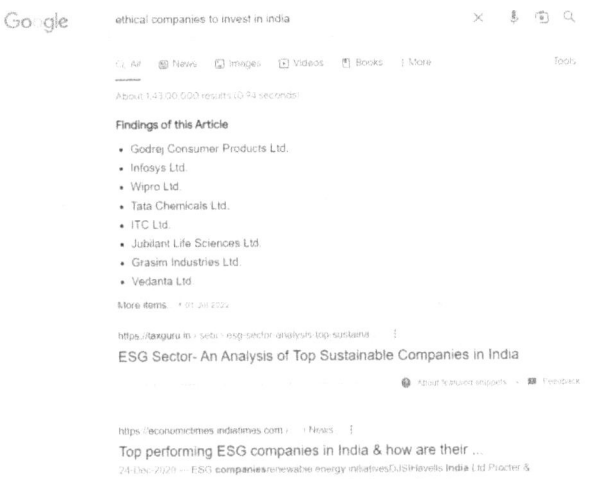

Figure: Screenshot of google to search for ethical companies to invest in India.

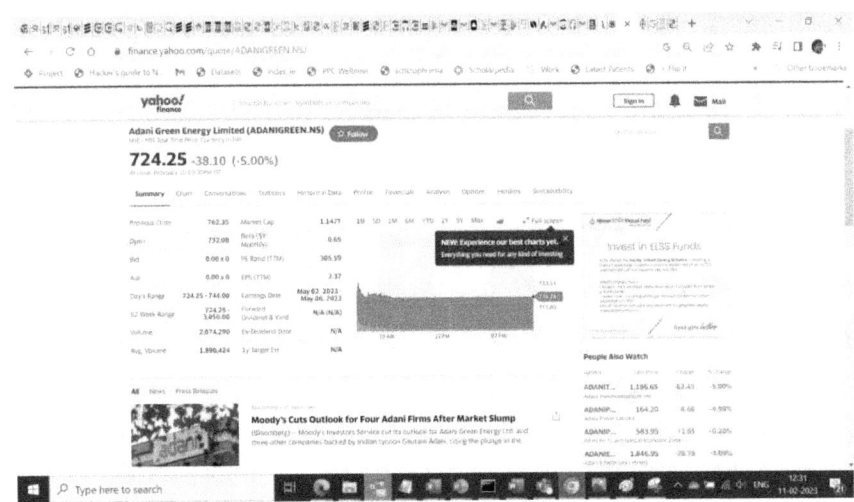

Figure: Screenshot showing analysis of a green firm on yahoo finance.

11.2 Money and investing websites

These include websites such as moneycontrol, yahoo finance, google finance etc. We can use such websites to keep track of the ESG and ethical related stocks and funds and also track the metrics such as P/E ratio, debt to equity and RoI, to decide whether the stock or fund is worth investing.

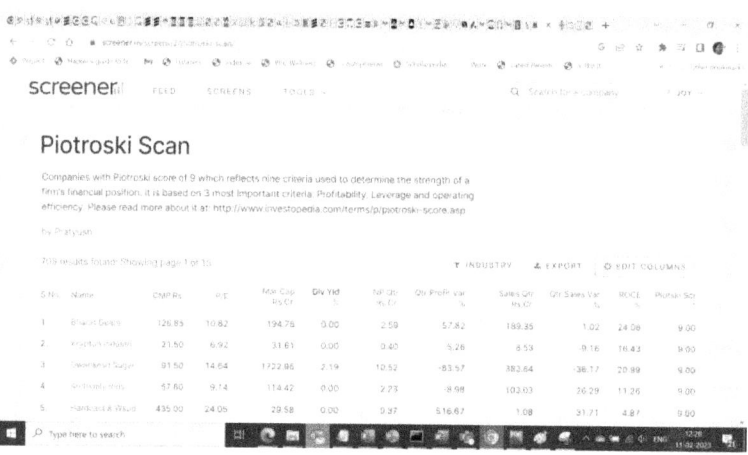

Figure: Screenshot of screener.in showing a screener that can be used to screen stocks as per some criteria or screening formulas based on metrics such as PE or ROI or dividend etc

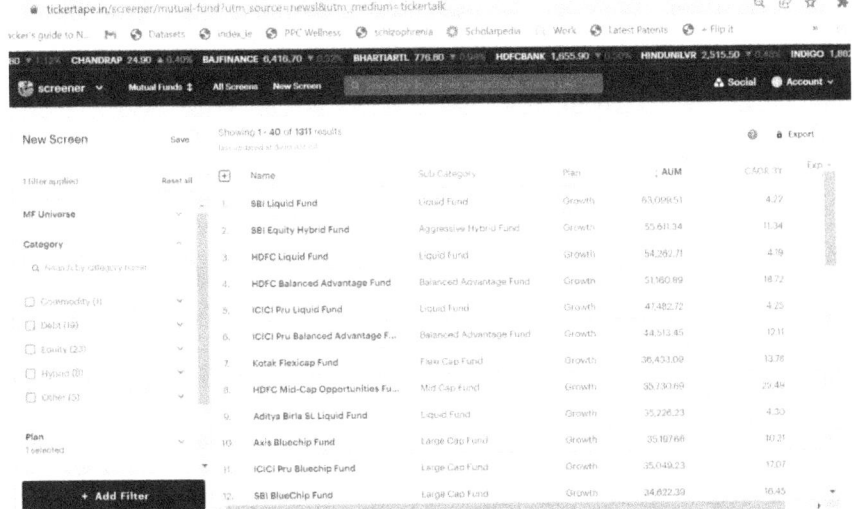

Figure: Screenshot of a screener in tickertape.in

We can also use screeners such as screener.in and tickertape.in for the same purpose.

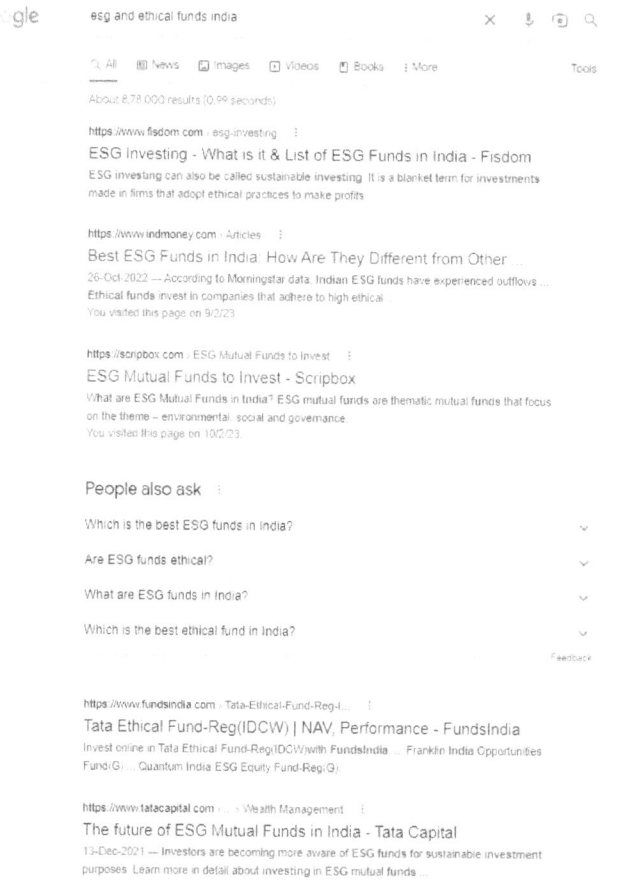

Figure: Search results on google for ESG and ethical funds.

11.3 Search engines

We can search for ethical investing in search engines like google or bing by searching for keywords relevant to ethical investing, such as "esg", "shariah" or "ethical".

Another option is to ask AI chatbots such as ChatGPT for questions related to ethical investing.

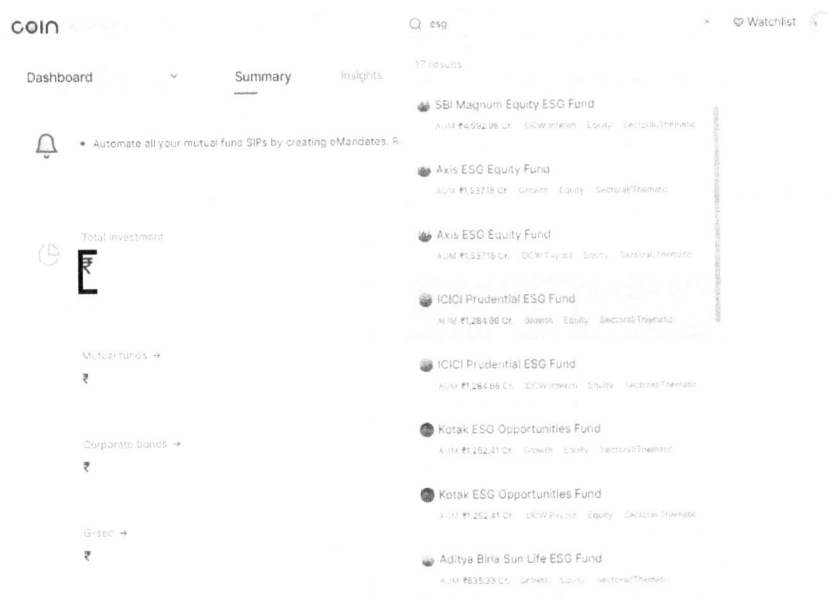

Figure: Screenshot of Zerodha coin showing the ESG mutual funds

11.4 Broker websites

Broker websites such as zerodha, groww, indmoney, ICICI direct or sharekhan can be similarly used to search for ESG or ethical funds and also analyze their performance.

11.5 Conclusion

In this chapter, we discussed some of the sources where we can get more information about ethical investing related funds and stock performance. Investors can use various tools and criteria to identify ethical investment opportunities. In the following chapters, we will explore specific investment types, including green energy and ESG mutual funds.

Chapter 12: Investing in Green Energy

Ethical investing includes various sectors, such as green energy, social impact investing, and Shariah-compliant funds. This and the following few chapters explore these opportunities in detail, starting with green energy.

In this chapter, we discuss some avenues for investing in green energy in India. Green energy is currently a major growth sector due to various incentives and tax concessions given by the government of India to this sector.

12.1 What are the investing avenues related to green energy

The main avenues related to green energy are as follows:

- Green stocks
- Green energy smallcases
- Sovereign Green bonds
- Fractional ownership of green assets

12.2 Green stocks

Green stocks and funds avoid companies that are related to pollution and include those companies that invest in green energy, clean water and other environmental causes.

Example: Adani Green Energy, https://www.adanigreenenergy.com/ which is a company focused on renewable green energy and operates large solar and wind farm projects.

Some listed companies in the Indian stock market (BSE and NSE) investing in renewable energy sources and other environment friendly practices include the following:

- Adani Green Energy

- Borosil Renewables: invests in renewable energy

- GAIL (India): invests in solar energy

- Indian Oil Corporation: invests in renewable energy

- JSW Energy: invests in renewable energy, mainly solar and wind projects

- Larsen & Toubro

- NTPC

- Reliance Industries: invests in renewable energy

- Tata Power Company

- Websol Energy System

- Suzlon energy

- Praj industries

- Gravita

- VaTech Wabag: related to water treatment

- Torrent power: is a power generation company that is investing in renewable energy

- GSPL

- IGL

- Ion exchange: water and waste management company

- Havells India Ltd (part of the Dow Jones sustainability index)

- Godrej consumer products (part of the Dow Jones sustainability index)

- Nestle India: has multiple sustainable projects

- P&G Hygiene & Healthcare: follows environmentally sustainable and socially responsible practices

- Colgate Palmolive India: has a variety of social projects with NGOs

- Page industries: has a sustainability culture

References:

https://www.equitymaster.com/detail.asp?date=12/09/2021&story=5&title=Indias-Top-Renewal-Energy-Stocks-Big-Returns-or-Boring-Returns

https://changestarted.com/green-companies-in-india-that-are-listed-on-stock-exchange/

https://www.ndtv.com/business/top-4-esg-stocks-to-add-to-your-watchlist-2699714

12.3 Green Energy smallcases

Another example is Green Energy related smallcases, which includes a basket of companies that are related to Green Energy. These can be searched in www.smallcase.com website. This is a portfolio of stocks, which will get benefit from the energy transition.

Energy transition refers to the global energy sector's shift from fossil-based systems of energy production and consumption — including oil, natural gas, and coal — to renewable energy sources like wind and solar, as well as other sources like biofuels.

Their major investment rationale is as follows:

Things like solar panel installations, electric vehicle sales are at record highs. ESG factors in Investing – Due to ESG factors in Investing, the energy transition will continue to increase in importance. Renewable electricity is increasingly cheaper than any new power capacity based on fossil fuels, according to a report by the International Renewable Energy Agency (IRENA). Climate change is set to be one of the top priorities for the world. More than a hundred countries have joined an alliance aiming for net-zero emissions by 2050.

The links are as follows, or else one can search for green energy in smallcase.com:

https://www.smallcase.com/smallcase/green-energy-portfolio-NIVTR_0001

https://www.smallcase.com/smallcase/green-energy-CHTSMO_0036

12.4 Sovereign Green Bonds (SGB)

The Government of India's Sovereign Green Bonds is another good way to invest in environment friendly initiatives by the government of India. These were introduced in the 2022-23 budget with the note *"As a part of the government's overall market borrowings in 2022-23, sovereign Green Bonds will be issued for mobilizing resources for green infrastructure. The proceeds will be deployed in public sector projects which help in reducing the carbon intensity of the economy."*

The aim of the SGB bond is to help in achieving India's green goals. These include five nectar elements (Panchamrit) of India's climate action: 1) Reach 500GW non-fossil energy capacity by 2030 2) 50 per cent of its energy requirements from renewable energy by 2030 3) Reduction of total projected carbon emissions by one billion tonnes from now to 2030 4) Reduction of the carbon intensity of the economy by 45 per cent by 2030, over 2005 levels 5) Achieving the target of net zero emissions by 2070.

The primary SGB bonds can be bought from RBI retail direct once they are issued (one announcement for their issuance was done in Jan 2023), from brokers such as zerodha or groww. They are usually sold in batches of 10, costing around Rupees 10000. They can also be bought in the secondary market from the brokers websites. Investment in these SGB bonds is usually low risk since they are guaranteed by the government.

Reference:
https://www.rbi.org.in/Scripts/BS_PressReleaseDisplay.aspx?prid=55164

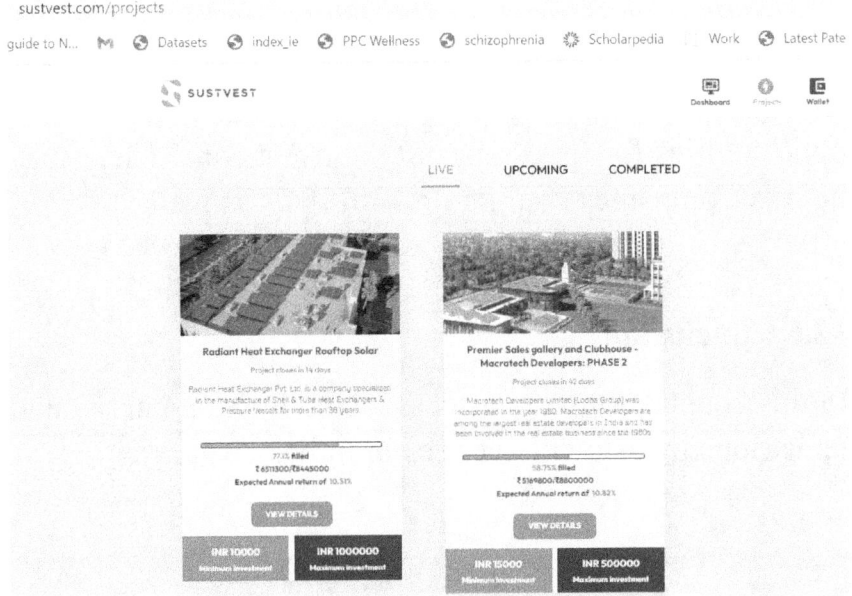

Figure: Screenshot of green energy projects such as project on solar energy panels, in sustvest.com website with the minimum investment

12.5 Fractional ownership of green assets

Another option is fractional ownership of Green assets. There are a few small companies working in the area that facilitate investments.

These include the following, besides others: Sustvest, which has multiple projects related to sustainability such as solar energy, where the investors can invest from as little as 5K or 10K rupees or higher. The website is https://www.sustvest.com/

Since green energy is a growing theme in India, one can find many startups also coming up on the theme of green energy and sustainability. For startups, one may search opportunities for investing in tykeinvest.com. There may be new companies coming up with IPOs as well.

12.6 Conclusion

In this chapter we have discussed about green energy and its various investment avenues in India.

Chapter 13: Social Investing

In this chapter we discuss socially responsible investing or social investing. These are microcredit websites that invest in villages and low-income communities, who often suffer from the problem of high interest loan sharks and moneylenders.

Socially responsible investing, or simply social investing, channels capital toward projects whose primary aim is to generate positive social outcomes. Rather than chasing only financial returns, social investors look for a double bottom line: measurable social benefit alongside sustainable, sometimes modest, financial gains. From microcredit in rural India to global health impact bonds, these approaches treat money as a tool for community development and shared prosperity.

Across the world, many low-income communities struggle with exploitative moneylenders who charge exorbitant rates. Access to fair, affordable credit can break cycles of poverty, enable small businesses to grow, and strengthen local economies. Social investing provides capital at reasonable terms, allowing individuals and communities to escape predatory debt and create self-sustaining livelihoods.

This is not philanthropy in the narrow sense; it is investing for social return, where the investor's reward includes both modest financial income and the satisfaction of measurable impact.

13.1 RangDe

Social investing is involved in empowering communities. Rang De is among India's most prominent social-investing platforms. Its website is https://rangde.in/

It provides low-interest loans to farmers, artisans and small entrepreneurs, groups traditionally underserved by banks and preyed upon by local moneylenders. Investors contribute small amounts that are pooled to fund these borrowers. As the loans are repaid, the funds can be recycled into new projects.

Participation is straightforward: investors open an online account, select projects, and track repayment and impact metrics. Returns are usually lower than commercial lending rates, but the social dividend, improved livelihoods and community resilience, is high.

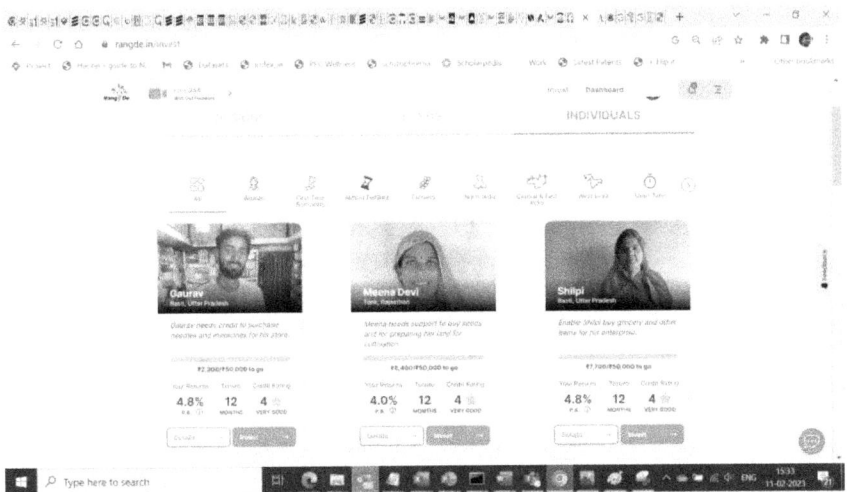

Figure: Screenshot of the RangDe website showing people from villages in different parts of India who need financing at a good interest rate for their small businesses.

13.2 International Microfinance platforms for social projects

113

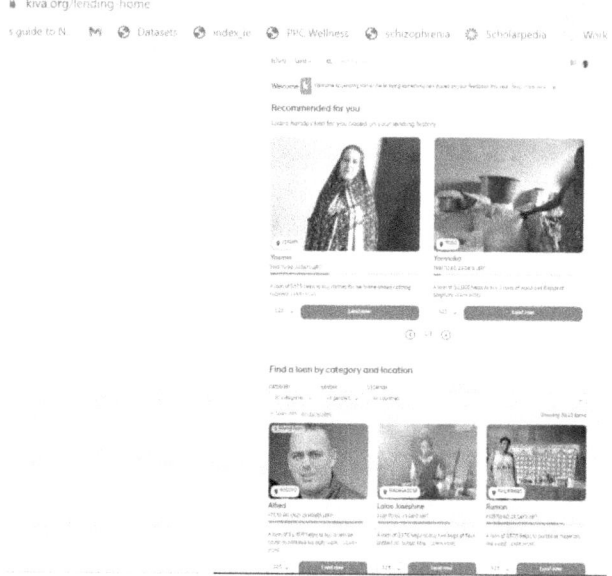

Figure: Screenshot of the kiva website showing available needs for microfinance lending

There are also a few foreign financing websites which include Indian projects such as kiva and lendwithcare.

Kiva is a U.S.-based non-profit (website www.kiva.org) that crowdsources microloans for agriculture, education, health care and small enterprise across more than 80 countries. Investors lend as little as USD 25 through PayPal and can recycle repayments into new loans.

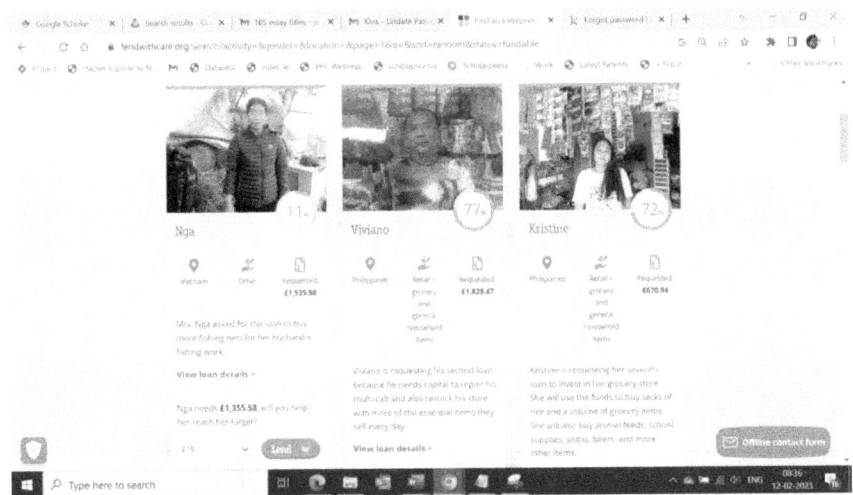

Figure: Screenshot of the lendwithcare website showing available needs for microfinance lending

The Lendwithcare website https://lendwithcare.org/ is a UK based website similar to RangDe and Kiva. It too sponsors social projects all over the world.

These platforms blend philanthropy and investment: the investor typically receives repayment of principal without interest, but the money continues to circulate, funding new entrepreneurs again and again.

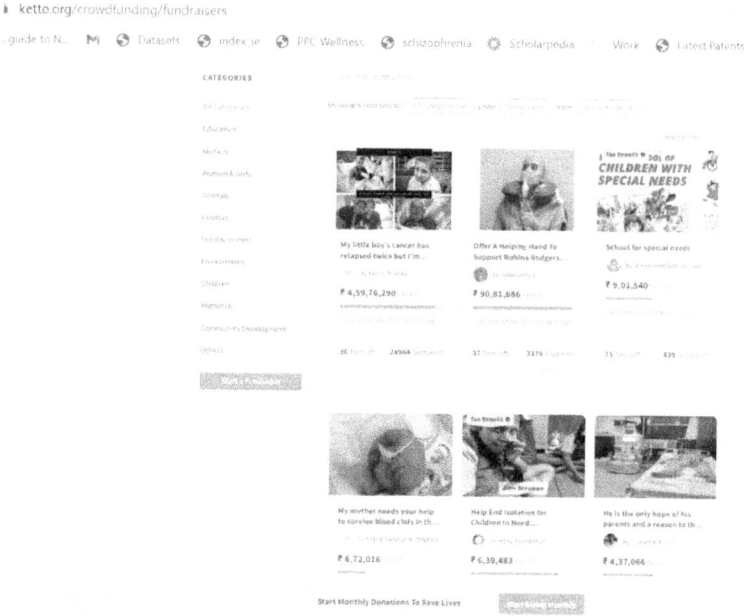

Figure: Screenshot of the Ketto website showing the currently running medical fundraisers.

13.3 Other social fundraising platforms based in India

There are a number of microfinance platforms and websites, as well as charities, which work in the development area and where one can invest or give directly. Donations to registered charities can be claimed against income tax section 80G.

Some of these include the following:

- Ketto: for medical fundraising, meeting medical bills of needy people. https://www.ketto.org/

- Milaap: Also for medical fundraising. https://milaap.org/crowdfunding/fundraisers

- Give.do: For donating and fundraising for various needy people and causes. https://give.do/

- Social for Action: Fundraising site https://socialforaction.com/

- Akshayapatra foundation: for donating meals to children and others https://www.akshayapatra.org/

Donations to many of these organizations qualify for tax deduction under Section 80G of the Indian Income Tax Act, allowing contributors to align generosity with fiscal planning.

13.4 Beyond Microfinance: New Forms of Social Investment

Social investing is evolving beyond classic microcredit. Below are some of the newer initiatives:

- **Development Impact Bonds (DIBs)**: investors fund programmes such as girls' education or public-health interventions and are repaid by donors or governments only if specific outcomes are achieved. The Educate Girls DIB in Rajasthan is a notable example.

- **Program-related investments**: These are foundations or development agencies provide low-interest loans or equity to social enterprises, expecting repayment but prioritising impact over profit.

- **Green and blue bonds with a social component**: These are fixed-income instruments where proceeds are earmarked for environmental or community projects, combining stable returns with measurable public benefit.

These instruments occupy a middle ground between pure philanthropy and conventional investing, offering varying degrees of financial return and social impact.

13.5 Evaluating and Monitoring Impact of social investing

Investing for social good requires the same discipline as traditional finance:

- Transparency and governance: check for audited accounts, clear mission statements and independent boards.

- Impact metrics: look for Social Return on Investment (SROI) or other measurable indicators such as number of children educated or litres of clean water delivered.

- Third-party verification: reputable platforms provide independent evaluations of their projects.

GuideStar India and Give.do provide comparative assessments of NGOs, helping investors identify credible partners and avoid "values-washing."

13.6 Conclusion

In this chapter, we have discussed social investing and fundraising platforms including rangde.in and others.

Social investing shows that money can be a force for inclusion and empowerment. Whether through RangDe loans to Indian farmers, a Kiva microloan to a Kenyan schoolteacher, or participation in a development impact bond, the investor's reward is twofold: modest financial return and the knowledge that their capital is building human capability and social resilience. In the spirit of Ken Honda's Happy Money, these investments allow money to circulate with gratitude and purpose, creating wealth measured not only in currency but in stronger, more equitable communities.

Chapter 14: Investing in environmental, social, and governance (ESG) mutual funds

In the world of ethical investing, few terms have gained as much attention as ESG: Environmental, Social, and Governance. What started as a niche movement has blossomed into a global trend, promising to transform not just how we invest, but how companies behave and how societies progress. Yet, beneath the marketing gloss and glowing reports, what does ESG truly mean for the thoughtful investor? How can we cut through the jargon and make choices that are both responsible and rewarding—personally, financially, and for the world?

In this chapter, we discuss some ESG funds which the interested investor can examine and invest in.

14.1 What is ESG, and Why Does It Matter?

At its core, ESG is a set of guiding principles that ask us to look beyond mere profit. It invites us to ask: How does a company treat the environment? Does it care for its workers, customers, and the communities where it operates? Is it governed with integrity, transparency, and fairness? These are not new questions—philosophers and reformers have pondered them for centuries—but ESG brings them squarely into the realm of investment decision-making.

Across India and the world, investors are waking up to the realization that the true value of a company goes far beyond quarterly earnings. Environmental factors push us to consider issues like climate change, water use, and waste management. Social criteria remind us of the importance of diversity, worker rights, safety, and how a company's actions ripple through society. Governance, the often-overlooked pillar, is about leadership, ethics, transparency, and how power is exercised and shared. Together, these dimensions form the heart of ESG.

14.2 The Indian Landscape: Regulation and Opportunity

India, like much of the world, is experiencing a surge of interest in ESG. The Securities and Exchange Board of India (SEBI) has set new benchmarks by requiring the largest listed companies to provide detailed Business Responsibility and Sustainability Reports. This is more than just bureaucratic box-ticking, it represents a fundamental shift in what is expected of India Inc. Mutual funds that market themselves as "ESG funds" must now adhere to stricter norms, explaining how they select, monitor, and engage with companies on sustainability issues.

Indian investors today have more choices than ever: from ESG mutual funds and ETFs to stocks of companies that are leading the way in green energy, inclusive hiring, or transparent governance. Tata Power's pivot to renewables, ITC's ambitious rural programs, and SBI's pioneering ESG funds offer glimpses into how Indian corporates are evolving. Yet, for every genuine leader, there are companies that pay only lip service, raising the spectre of "greenwashing"—the practice of exaggerating or faking sustainability credentials.

14.3 ESG criteria

The environmental social and governance (ESG) criteria include the company's culture, risk appetite and management. They include environmental, social, and governance standards. The company needs to be environment-friendly in their operations, ethical in its financial disclosures and can sustain the highest governance standards to be included under the criteria.

- **Environmental criteria** may include factors such as the carbon footprint, resource usage, waste management, and efforts to mitigate climate change by the company.

- **Social criteria** may include factors such as labor practices, diversity and inclusion policies, and human rights record of the company.

- **Governance criteria** may include factors such as the company's board diversity, executive compensation structure, and transparency in financial reporting.

14.4 Measuring Impact: From Numbers to Narratives

For the individual investor, the ESG landscape can feel both exciting and confusing. How do you know if an investment is truly making a difference? This is where measurement comes in. A new ecosystem of ESG ratings, scorecards, and impact frameworks, such as the Global Reporting Initiative (GRI), IRIS+, SASB standards, and ratings from agencies like CRISIL or MSCI, aims to provide clarity. Yet, no system is perfect, and standards can vary between countries and rating providers.

ESG Ratings: These ratings are given by agencies such as MSCI, Sustainalytics, Refinitiv, and Indian agencies like CRISIL.

Impact Measurement Frameworks include the following:

- Global Reporting Initiative (GRI)

- IRIS+ (Impact Reporting and Investment Standards)

- SASB (Sustainability Accounting Standards Board)

- GIIRS (Global Impact Investing Rating System)

Real impact is best measured not just in numbers, but in stories and evidence: a reduction in a company's carbon emissions, a new maternity benefit for its workers, a commitment to independent board oversight. Many funds and companies now publish annual impact reports. Retail investors, in turn, are learning to read beyond the headlines—studying fund fact sheets, ESG ratings, and disclosures on company websites, and asking hard questions about how investments are monitored and evaluated.

14.5 Critiques, Challenges, and the Limits of ESG

No movement is without its critics. Some argue that ESG funds underperform traditional ones or that ethical screens are arbitrary and inconsistent. Others point to the challenge of balancing environmental, social, and governance priorities—what happens, for instance, when a company excels environmentally but fails on labour rights, or vice versa? Perhaps the sharpest critique is that of greenwashing: when companies or funds talk the ESG talk but do not walk the walk, misleading investors and undermining trust.

These criticisms are important. They remind us that ESG is not a silver bullet and that vigilance is required. The antidote lies in scepticism, due diligence, and a demand for transparency. Investors should look for clear, quantifiable data, insist on third-party verification, and avoid investments that rely on vague promises or unverifiable claims.

14.6 ESG for Every Investor

Whether you are just starting your investment journey, planning for retirement, or managing a family's wealth, there is a place for ESG in your portfolio. Beginners may find comfort in diversified ESG funds or index funds. NRIs and global Indians can tap into both Indian and international ESG opportunities. Retirees looking for stability might consider green bonds or conservative ESG debt funds. For young professionals, SIPs into ESG-focused funds can plant seeds for a sustainable future, financially and environmentally.

For those eager to explore further, organizations such as SEBI, GIIN, CEEW, and Morningstar provide reliable guidance and data. Fintech platforms like Groww and Zerodha offer ESG filters for retail investors, while independent research agencies and NGOs track corporate performance and controversies.

14.7 Companies meeting the ESG criteria

For example, for the SBI Magnum Equity ESG Fund, the companies meeting the ESG criteria include the following:

- Housing Development Finance Corporation Ltd.

- ICICI Bank Ltd.

- HDFC Bank Ltd.

- Infosys Ltd.

- Axis Bank Ltd.

- Larsen & Toubro Ltd.

- Ultratech Cement Ltd.

- State Bank of India

- Mahindra & Mahindra Ltd.

- Kotak Mahindra Bank Ltd.

- Britannia Industries Ltd.

- Maruti Suzuki India Ltd.

- Eicher Motors Ltd.

- Tata Consultancy Services Ltd.

14.8 List of ESG mutual funds

There are a number of mutual funds that are focused on ESG criteria companies and are usually identified with the term ESG in their title or description. These can be invested through any of the stock brokers or also from the netbanking sites of most banks like Kotak, SBI and ICICI.

A list of ESG mutual funds available for investors in India is as follows:

- **SBI Magnum Equity ESG Fund**: https://www.sbimf.com/sbimf-scheme-details/SBI-Magnum-Equity-ESG-Fund-1 invests mainly in companies that follow good ESG practices. An open-ended Equity scheme investing in companies following the EGS theme.

- **Axis ESG Equity Fund** https://www.axismf.com/mutual-funds/equity-funds/axis-esg-equity-fund/ee-gp/regular An Open-ended equity scheme investing in companies demonstrating sustainable practices across Environment, Social and Governance (ESG) theme

- **ICICI Prudential ESG Fund** https://www.icicidirect.com/mutual-funds/nav-details/icici-pru-esg-fund-(g)-41670 This is a fund that encourages Sustainable Investing by investing in Companies that follow the ESG theme.

- **Kotak ESG Opportunities Fund** https://www.kotakmf.com/Products/funds/equity-funds/Kotak-ESG-Opportunities-Fund/Dir-G An Open-ended equity scheme which follows the Environment, Social and Governance (ESG) theme with the flexibility of investing across market capitalization.

- **Aditya Birla Sun Life ESG Fund** https://mutualfund.adityabirlacapital.com/wealth-creation-solutions/aditya-birla-sun-life-esg-fund The objective is to generate long-term capital appreciation by investing in a diversified basket of companies following Environmental, Social and Governance (ESG) theme.

- **Invesco India ESG Equity Fund** https://www.invescomutualfund.com/ This has investments in companies which are selected based on Environmental, Social & Governance (ESG) criteria.

- **Quant ESG Equity Fund** https://quantmutual.com/equity/quant-esg-equity-fund This fund has the objective to generate long term capital appreciation by investing in a diversified portfolio of companies demonstrating sustainable practices across Environmental, Social and Governance (ESG) parameters.

- **Quantum India ESG Equity Fund**
  https://www.quantumamc.com/equity-funds/quantum-india-esg-equity-fund The Quantum India ESG Equity Fund invests in companies that are focused on conserving the environment, on positively impacting communities that they operate in, and conducting business ethically. These sustainable businesses are not only environmentally and socially responsible but also make great sense as investments as you look to build wealth over the long term.

- **Mirae Asset Nifty 100 ESG Sector Leaders Fund of Fund**
  https://www.miraeassetmf.co.in/mutual-fund-scheme/fof-and-index-funds/mirae-asset-nifty-100-esg-sector-leaders-fund-of-fund As per investment objective, the scheme will predominantly invest in units of Mirae Asset ESG Sector Leaders ETF, the portfolio of which shall mostly be based on stocks forming part of Nifty100 ESG Sector Leaders Index.

New mutual funds and NFOs keep coming up all the time. It is important to keep track on them and especially their performance, via one's broker such as Zerodha.

14.9 Looking Forward: The Future of ESG Investing

ESG investing in India is at an inflection point. Regulatory scrutiny is increasing, impact standards are tightening, and the demand from a new generation of investors is reshaping priorities. The role of technology will only grow, making impact measurement more precise, but also introducing new risks. As India integrates further with global supply chains and capital markets, ESG norms will converge with world standards, raising the bar for all participants.

What remains unchanged is the core principle: that investing is not only about growing personal wealth, but about shaping the world we leave behind. ESG offers a path for investors to be agents of positive change, nudging companies and markets toward responsibility, resilience, and renewal.

14.10 Case Studies: Learning from Success and Failure

Consider Tata Power, which has shifted its business model from coal-heavy operations to renewables, publishing clear goals and transparent progress updates. Or SBI's ESG fund, which spells out its selection criteria and exclusions. Globally, Tesla is often lauded for its environmental innovation but criticized for governance and labour practices, highlighting the complexity of ESG scoring. Beyond Meat demonstrates how a company can align environmental and social impact, even if financial performance is volatile.

These examples reveal both the potential and the messiness of ESG investing. There are no perfect companies, but there are meaningful distinctions between those striving for improvement and those merely painting themselves green.

14.11 Summary Table: ESG Investing at a glance

Aspect	What to Check/Do	Common Pitfalls
Fund Selection	Use verified ESG ratings, review impact	Vague mandates, greenwashing
Company Choice	Read BRSR/ESG disclosures	Relying only on marketing
Impact Measure	Look for quantifiable impact, third-party	No reporting, unclear data
Regulation	Check SEBI/Global rules	Outdated or ignored rules
Tech Tools	Use fintech ESG trackers, research AI use	Trusting black-box ratings

14.12 Conclusion

In this chapter, we have discussed a few types of ESG mutual fund investments.

In a world increasingly defined by uncertainty and interconnectedness, ESG investing challenges us to think bigger—to see money not only as a tool for individual advancement but as a lever for societal and planetary good. It is a journey of curiosity, courage, and continuous learning. By demanding transparency, measuring what matters, and investing with heart as well as mind, you can help create a future where prosperity and purpose walk hand in hand.

Chapter 15: Shariah compliant investing

In this chapter we discuss avenues for investing in Shariah compliant funds, which can also be seen in the context of broader ethical investing. These funds are as per certain ethical criteria and open to all who are interested in an ethical framework for investing, not just Muslims.

15.1 Eligibility criteria for selection of stocks in the Nifty50 Shariah index

The eligibility criteria for selection of stocks for Nifty50 Shariah index includes the following:

- The current constituents of the Nifty 50 index are screened for Shariah compliance, those that are compliant form the Nifty50 Shariah.

- The company should have a listing history of 6 months. A company which comes out with an IPO will be eligible for inclusion in the index, if it fulfills the normal eligibility criteria for the index for a 3 month period instead of a 6 month period.

- Stocks that meet above mentioned criteria and are also Shariah compliant form part of Nifty50 Shariah Index.

- Weightage of each stock in the index is calculated based on its free-float market capitalization such that no single stock shall be more than 33% and weightage of top 3 stocks cumulatively shall not be more than 62% at the time of rebalancing.

These screen stocks with more than a minimum market capitalization where the amount of income from interest, trade receivables and debt is low. The companies should have cash to total assets ratio less than a threshold, debt to company value also less than a threshold (usually 33%), interest income to total income is very low and there is no involvement of the company in weapons, narcotic drugs etc.

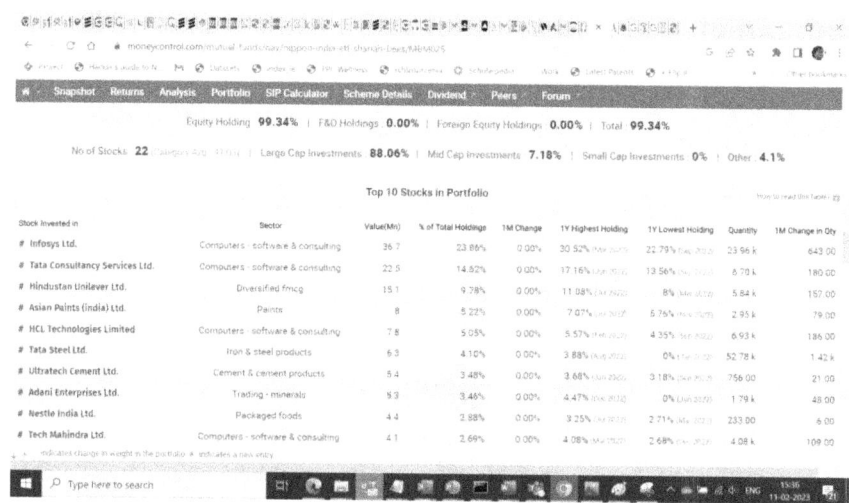

Figure: Screenshots from the moneycontrol website showing some top stocks in the SHARIAHBEES (Nippon India ETF Nifty 50 Shariah Bees) portfolio

15.2 List of Shariah compliant funds

A list of Shariah compliant mutual funds available in India is as follows:

- **Tata**   **Ethical**   **Fund**
  https://www.tatamutualfund.com/products/tata-ethical-fund This invests mainly in companies that are Shariah compliant. Tata Ethical Fund is an open-ended equity fund which invests in a diversified equity portfolio based on principles of Shariah. The investment objective of the scheme is to provide medium to long-term capital gains by investing in Shariah compliant equity and equity-related instruments of well-researched value and growth-oriented companies.

- **Nippon India ETF Nifty 50 Shariah BeES**
  https://www.moneycontrol.com/mutual-funds/nav/nippon-india-etf-shariah-bees/MBM025 This ETF (exchange traded fund) invests in companies selected from Nifty50 Shariah Index. The investment objective of Nippon India ETF Nifty 50 Shariah BeES (Formerly Nippon India ETF Shariah BeES) is to provide returns that, before expenses, closely correspond to the total returns of the Securities as represented by the Nifty50 Shariah Index by investing in Securities which are constituents of the Nifty50 Shariah Index in the same proportion as in the Index.

- **Taurus**   **ethical**   **fund**
  https://www.taurusmutualfund.com/taurus-ethical-fund This is a Shariah compliant fund. Investors looking for suitable investment opportunities that

comply with Shariah norms should look to invest in the Taurus Ethical fund with a Medium to Long term investment horizon. It is a socially responsible form of investing. The S&P BSE 500 Shariah Index is used as the benchmark for comparing the performance of this Scheme.

- **The Wealth Company Ethical Fund (India)**: Launched in September 2025, The Wealth Company Ethical Fund positions itself under SEBI's newly recognized "ethical funds" subcategory, with a guiding principle drawn from ahimsa (non-violence): invest in businesses that do no harm to living creatures, society, or the environment. Its exclusion list is broad: alcohol, gambling, tobacco, meat & poultry, leather, pesticides, insecticides, and other "sin" industries are disqualified from the portfolio. The scheme seeks long-term capital growth via actively managed equity holdings in ethically compliant companies. With a minimum lump sum of ₹1,000, SIP starting at ₹250, and an exit load of 1% if redeemed within 30 days, it is designed to balance accessibility and discipline. As one of India's freshest forays into formally labelled ethical mutual funds, it is a useful case study in how the "happy money" sensibility might find expression in mainstream finance.

15.3 Conclusion

In this chapter we have considered avenues for Shariah compliant investing. As mentioned, these funds can be considered by all people who are looking at a broad and verifiable ethical framework.

Chapter 16: Wellness related companies and funds listed on NSE and BSE

In this chapter we look at some wellness related companies that are listed in BSE And NSE. Wellness may be considered as a part of ethical investing since it is related to overall well-being.

16.1 Listed wellness related companies

Some of the wellness related companies listed in NSE and BSE include the following:

- **Dabur India**: Dabur is one of the best known ayurvedic brands in India. It was set up in 1884. It manufactures a number of products including Dabur Chyawanprash. Its website is https://www.dabur.com/

- **Patanjali**: It is an ayurveda company under yoga guru Baba Ramdev. It manufactures a range of affordable ayurveda related products. Its website is https://www.patanjaliayurved.net/

- **Zydus Wellness**: It produces health food products, skincare and other wellness related products including well known brands such as Glucon-D,

Complan and Nycil. Its website is https://www.zyduswellness.com/

- **Kerala Ayurveda**: It manufactures ayurvedic medicines, has an online ayurvedic store and a number of services such as Vaidya consultations and ayurveda retreats. Its website is https://www.keralaayurveda.biz/

- **Tiaan Consumer** (Tiaan Ayurvedic and He): It is a small cap company that manufactures ayurvedic products. Its website is https://tiaanstore.com/

- **Rajnish Wellness**: It started as a teleshopping venture and grown into a listed company with various wellness products. Its website is https://rajnishwellness.com/

References:

https://vibcare.co.in/top-10-ayurvedic-companies-in-india/

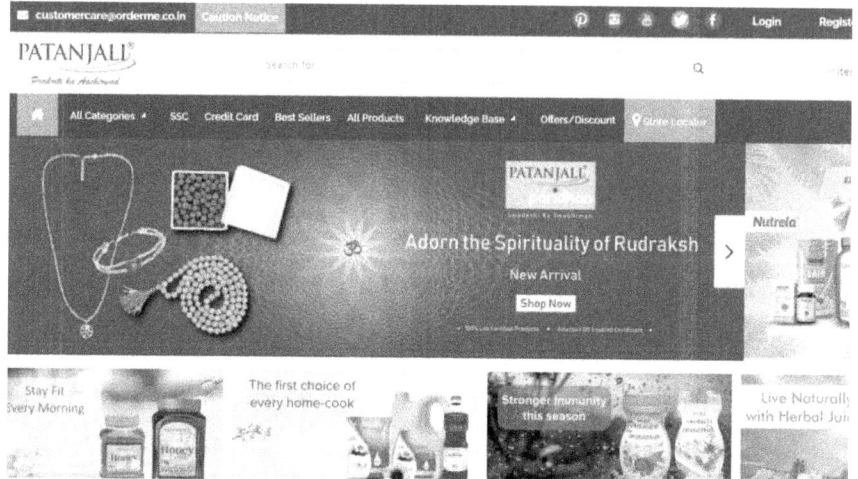

Figure: Screenshot from website of Patanjali ayurveda

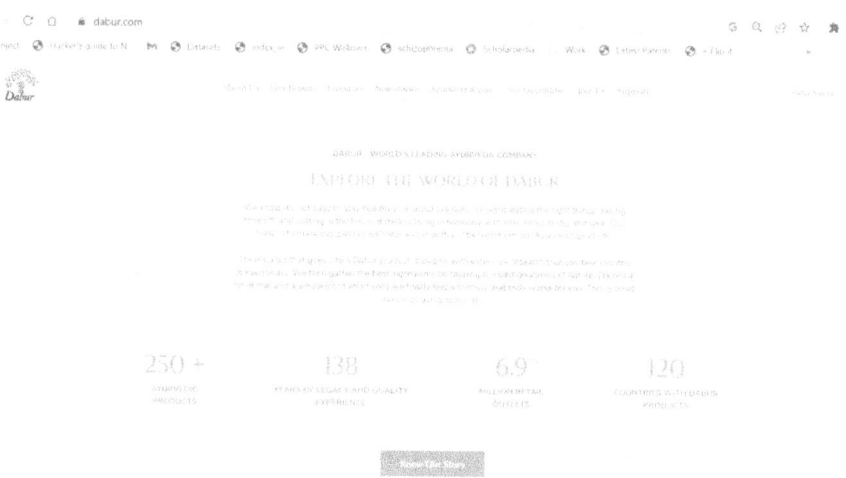

Figure: Screenshot from Dabur website

16.2 Healthcare mutual funds

There are also a few healthcare related mutual funds where one can invest in. Their performance can be tracked by searching for terms such as pharma and healthcare in mutual funds listings at the broker websites such as zerodha.

Some of these healthcare related mutual funds include the following:

- SBI Healthcare opportunities fund

- UTI healthcare fund

- Tata India Pharma and healthcare fund

- Nippon India Pharma fund

- DSP healthcare fund

- UTI healthcare fund

- ICICI Prudential Pharma Healthcare and Diagnostics (P.H.D) Fund

- Mirae Asset healthcare fund

- Aditya Birla Sun Life Pharma & Healthcare Fund

- IDBI healthcare fund

16.3 Conclusion

In this chapter, we have discussed a few wellness related, ayurveda related and nutrition related companies and mutual funds listed on the Indian stock market.

Chapter 17: Ethical Investing for different profiles

Ethical investing is not a one-size-fits-all approach. People of different ages, backgrounds, incomes, and aspirations will naturally have different investment needs, time horizons, and levels of risk tolerance. What unites them is the desire to grow wealth responsibly while contributing positively to society and the environment. This chapter is a practical guide to tailoring ethical investing strategies for various investor profiles in India and beyond.

17.1 The New Investor and the Curious Beginner

Profile: A young adult, student, or professional just starting their financial journey, possibly with limited capital and little investment experience.

Challenges facing the new investors include the following:

- Overwhelmed by jargon and too many options.

- Unsure how to begin without risking too much.

- Wants to make a difference, but doesn't want to fall for "greenwashing."

Recommended Approach:

Start with Small, Regular Investments: SIPs (Systematic Investment Plans) in ethical or ESG mutual funds or ETFs allow beginners to invest as little as ₹100–₹500 per month, building the habit and growing confidence.

Use Robo-Advisors and Investment Apps: Platforms like Groww, Zerodha, or Kuvera now offer ESG filters, making it easier to select ethical funds.

Stick to Diversified Funds: Avoid the risk of putting all your eggs in one basket by choosing diversified ESG funds rather than picking individual "ethical" stocks.

Learn as You Go: Use resources—blogs, podcasts, books, and fund factsheets—to build your understanding of impact, risk, and transparency.

Example:
Riya, a 24-year-old software engineer in Bangalore, starts a monthly SIP in an ESG index fund and follows news on environmental and social issues, learning how her money is connected to the wider world.

17.2 The Middle-Class Indian Family

Profile: A working couple balancing household expenses, children's education, elder care, and the dream of home ownership.

Challenges facing the middle class family when it comes to ethical investing include:

- Limited investable surplus after living costs.
- Concerned about safety, returns, and social impact.
- Needs investments that match life goals and family values.

Recommended approach:

Prioritize Financial Security: Maintain an emergency fund and insurance before allocating significant amounts to investments.

Blend Traditional and Ethical Options: Alongside PPF, FDs, or gold, allocate a portion to ESG funds, green bonds, or social impact fixed income schemes.

Explore Government and Bank-Led Social Bonds: SBI, NABARD, and other institutions periodically issue green or social bonds with transparent use-of-proceeds.

Consider Children's Future: Look for child-focused investment products that promote social responsibility, such as Sukanya Samriddhi accounts with ethical overlays.

Example:
Sandeep and Neha, both teachers, invest part of their annual bonus in a green bond and teach their children the

basics of financial ethics using stories and online resources.

17.3 The Non-Resident Indian (NRI)

Profile: An Indian living abroad, interested in supporting social and environmental progress back home while growing their savings.

Challenges facing NRIs when it comes to ethical investing include the following:

- Navigating regulations (NRE/NRO accounts, FEMA, tax).

- Accessing trustworthy products remotely.

- Currency risks and tax differences.

Approach:

Use Reputed Banks and Platforms: Stick to established banks, mutual fund platforms, and SEBI-registered investment advisors for ESG or SRI products.

Diversify Globally: Consider global ESG funds and ETFs listed on US, UK, or Singapore exchanges, as well as Indian options accessible to NRIs.

Monitor Impact Remotely: Use online tools and annual reports to keep track of both returns and impact.

Example:

Anjali, an NRI doctor in the US, invests in both a US-listed ESG ETF and an SBI ESG fund in India via her NRE account, tracking impact through fund disclosures.

17.4 The Young Professional with Ambition

Profile: Someone early in their career, willing to take some risks, with a desire for both returns and purpose.

Challenges facing young professionals include:

- Risk of short-term speculation.

- Temptation to chase the latest "trendy" investments.

- Balancing rapid wealth creation with long-term goals.

Recommended approach:

Focus on Growth and Innovation: Invest in ESG funds with exposure to new sectors—clean tech, healthcare, financial inclusion.

Start a Side Portfolio: Allocate a small portion (5–10%) for direct investments in ethical startups via crowdfunding platforms or impact investing networks.

Automate Investing: Use SIPs or auto-invest features to remain consistent even in volatile markets.

Engage with Community: Join online or local impact investing groups, attend webinars, and network to stay informed and inspired.

Example:
Amit, a 29-year-old fintech analyst, puts most of his investments in ESG index funds, but also supports a local clean water social enterprise via a crowdfunding site.

17.5 The Retiree or Pre-Retiree

Profile: An individual nearing or in retirement, seeking stable income, capital preservation, and peace of mind.

Challenges facing retirees when it comes to ethical investing include the following:

- Low tolerance for volatility or risk of loss.

- Need for steady cash flow.

- Desire to leave a positive legacy.

Recommended Approach:

Choose Conservative ESG related Debt Funds and Green Bonds: These often provide more stability than equity-oriented funds.

Consider Dividend-Paying ESG Stocks: Some companies with strong ESG credentials pay regular dividends.

Look for Social Impact Fixed Deposits: Some banks and NBFCs offer special deposits with clear impact reporting.

Plan for Philanthropy: Explore options for giving—via donor-advised funds, charitable trusts, or direct support to social enterprises as part of estate planning.

Example:
Mr. Sharma, a retired PSU manager, invests in a mix of green bonds, an ESG debt fund, and a charitable trust supporting rural education.

17.6 The Women Investor

Profile: A woman seeking financial independence and a voice in household or personal investment decisions.

Challenges facing women in ethical investing include:

- Gender gap in financial literacy and confidence.

- Time constraints due to multiple roles.

- Stereotypes about risk aversion.

Recommended Approach:

Read books on investing focused on women such as Girls that Invest by Simran Kaur, Smart Women Finish Rich by David Bach, Rich Women by Kim Kiyosaki, Clever Girl Finance by Bola Sokunbi.

Join Women-Focused Investment Platforms: Communities like LXME and Women on Wealth offer financial education with an ethical lens.

Invest in Gender-Lens Funds: Some mutual funds and ETFs specifically support women-led businesses or companies promoting gender equality.

Encourage Inter-Generational Dialogue: Foster financial conversations among women in the family—mothers, daughters, sisters.

Example:
Priya, a small business owner, invests in a gender-lens ESG fund and mentors other women through an online investing group.

17.7 The Values-Driven HNI and Institutional Investor

Profile: High net-worth individuals, family offices, and institutions aiming for legacy, impact, and reputational benefit.

Challenges facing HNIs include:

- Need for large, diversified, and sometimes bespoke investments.

- Higher expectations for impact reporting and transparency.

- Balancing philanthropy with financial performance.

Recommended approach:

Direct Impact Investing: Invest in private equity, venture funds, or direct projects focused on clean energy, health, education, and financial inclusion.

Mandate ESG Integration: Require fund managers and advisors to apply ESG screens across all asset classes.

Commission Impact Reports: Insist on robust, third-party impact measurement and reporting.

Champion Corporate Governance: Use shareholder power to influence better practices in companies.

Example:
The Rao family office allocates a portion of its portfolio to direct investments in Indian climate tech startups, commissioning annual independent impact reports.

17.8 For All: Tips for Every Ethical Investor

Know Your "Why": Be clear about your values and what ethical investing means to you.

Start Small, Grow Gradually: Begin with manageable amounts, increasing allocation as your comfort grows.

Diversify and Rebalance: Mix different asset types and review your portfolio regularly.

Beware of Greenwashing: Scrutinize products and claims; look for transparency and third-party verification.

Stay Informed: Read, attend webinars, join communities, and keep learning.

17.9 Conclusion

No matter your age, occupation, income, or aspirations, ethical investing can be a meaningful part of your financial story. The specifics will differ—how much you invest, your mix of products, your appetite for risk—but the guiding principles remain: seek transparency, align your money with your values, and let your wealth contribute to a fairer and more sustainable world. In doing so, you not only build financial security for yourself and your loved ones but also leave a legacy that extends far beyond your own lifetime.

Chapter 18: Practical Toolkit for the Ethical Investor

The preceding chapters have traced the philosophy and practice of ethical investing, from Ken Honda's "happy money" to global ESG markets and impact philanthropy. Yet good intentions need structure. This chapter gathers the most useful tools and checklists so that values-driven finance becomes a concrete, repeatable practice rather than an occasional impulse.

18.1 Drafting Your Ethical Investment Policy Statement

A written Ethical Investment Policy Statement (EIPS) serves as your compass when markets are volatile or when fashionable causes tempt you to chase headlines. It should include:

- Purpose: the social or environmental outcomes you wish to support (for example, renewable energy, affordable healthcare, elder care).

- Financial goals: target returns, time horizon, and risk tolerance.

- Exclusions and priorities: industries or practices you will avoid (tobacco, arms, exploitative labour) and those you will favour.

- Asset allocation: the mix of equities, bonds, real estate, and philanthropic giving.

- Review schedule: how often you will revisit and update the statement, typically once a year.

Having these principles in writing provides clarity and protects against emotional decision-making.

18.2 Screening and Due Diligence Checklist

Before buying an ESG fund, green bond, or impact product, examine:

1. Screening methodology: Does the fund simply exclude certain industries, or does it positively select best-in-class performers?

2. Third-party verification: Are there independent ESG ratings or second-party opinions (e.g., MSCI, Sustainalytics, ISS)?

3. Impact reporting: Does the issuer publish measurable outcomes—tonnes of carbon avoided, number of patients treated, hectares of forest restored?

4. Governance and transparency: Look for audited accounts, clear use-of-proceeds statements, and accessible annual reports.

This checklist helps avoid greenwashing, which is the term that refers to marketing sustainability without delivering it.

18.3 Core Resources and Platforms

For India ethical investing:

- SEBI disclosures and mutual fund fact sheets.

- Platforms such as RangDe for domestic microfinance and Give.do or GuideStar India for charity evaluation.

- RBI's Liberalised Remittance Scheme (LRS) guidelines for overseas investment.

For International ethical investing

- ESG ratings agencies: MSCI ESG Research, Sustainalytics, FTSE4Good.

- Global impact databases: GIIN's ImpactBase, Principles for Responsible Investment (PRI) signatory lists.

- Micro-lending platforms such as Kiva or Lendwithcare.

Use these sources to cross-check claims and build a globally diversified yet ethically sound portfolio.

18.4 Building a Balanced Ethical Portfolio

A practical approach for building an ethical portfolio might include the following:

- Core holdings: low-cost ESG index funds or ETFs for global equity exposure.

- Fixed income: a mix of domestic and international green or blue bonds for stability and environmental impact.

- Impact slice: 5–10 % of investible surplus for high-impact vehicles such as development impact bonds, microfinance, or social enterprises.

- Philanthropic allocation: a fixed percentage of income, treated as a parallel asset class, for direct giving.

The precise mix will depend on your risk tolerance and life goals, but this structure ensures that both financial and ethical priorities are represented.

18.5 Habits for Sustainable Success

Some sustainable success habits include the following:

- Automate savings, investments and donations to make them routine.

- Schedule periodic reviews, quarterly or annually, rather than reacting to daily market noise.

- Pair financial metrics with impact narratives: track the social and environmental benefits alongside portfolio returns.

These habits reinforce the mindset described in earlier chapters: money flowing with gratitude and purpose.

18.6 From Intention to Practice

Ethical investing is not a single transaction but an ongoing discipline. This toolkit is meant to be adapted, such as expanded as new products, ratings and impact measures evolve. By combining clear principles, rigorous due diligence and simple habits, you can ensure that every rupee or dollar you save, spend or give becomes part of a larger story: money that grows while helping the world to flourish.

Chapter 19: Conclusion

In this book, we have briefly discussed the meaning of ethical investing and explored some of the investment avenues in India where one can invest ethically.

Ethical investing is much more than a set of rules or financial techniques. As explored throughout this book, it is a way of relating to money and the world that honours both practical realities and our deepest values. Whether we draw guidance from ancient scriptures, Greek and Western philosophy, behavioural science, or the personal stories of investors and activists, the message is clear: how we earn, save, invest, and give matters—not only for our own well-being, but for the society and planet we share.

19.1 Integrating Wisdom from Many Sources

From the teachings of Buddhism, Christianity, Islam, Hinduism, and Judaism, to the insights of Aristotle, Seneca, Adam Smith, and modern psychologists, we learn that money is best seen as a tool—a means to support a flourishing, just, and meaningful life. The philosophies explored in these chapters remind us to seek balance, practice gratitude, and cultivate generosity. Money can serve as a source of anxiety and division, but also as a force for healing, creativity, and social good.

19.2 The Psychology of Money: A Lifelong Journey

Behavioural economics and modern psychology reveal that our relationship with money is deeply emotional and often unconscious. Recognizing our personal "money scripts," practicing mindfulness, and developing healthy habits, such as automating savings, focusing on "enough," and investing in line with our values, can bring lasting peace of mind. The wisdom of thinkers like Morgan Housel, Ken Honda, and Lynne Twist shows that real wealth is measured not just in numbers, but in contentment, freedom, and positive impact.

19.3 Practical Steps for the Ethical Investor

Ethical investing is accessible to everyone, regardless of income or background. We can start by clarifying your values and understanding the impact of your financial decisions. Use the tools and strategies outlined in this book such as green and social investment vehicles, mutual funds, index funds, SIPs, and conscious spending, to build a portfolio that reflects both our personal goals and our hopes for a better world. Let us remember, consistency and patience are as important as technical expertise.

19.4 A Mindful and Abundant Future

As we move forward, let us remember that every rupee, dollar, or euro we invest is a vote for the kind of future we wish to see. Let our investments flow with gratitude and intention. Let us embrace the abundance mindset, thank your money as it comes and goes, support causes that uplift others, and cultivate generosity in all areas of our life.

The journey of ethical investing is ongoing. Markets change, circumstances shift, and new opportunities emerge. Yet the core principles, those of wisdom, compassion, self-awareness, and purpose, remain timeless. By integrating these lessons into our financial life, we can achieve not only material security, but also the satisfaction of knowing that our money is aligned with our heart and our hopes for the world.

Ethical investing is only one part of a lifestyle that displays a healthy relationship with money, as a means of exchanging positive energy with the people around us, so that we can contribute to building a better world for everyone. Investing in ESG and ethical funds and social investing are all steps towards this goal.

If all of us take concrete steps towards ethical investing by doing a periodic ethical audit of our investments and ensuring that we are contributing towards saving rather than destroying this planet, then not only will there be benefits for ourselves and future generations towards building a sustainable and more livable happier world, but the returns we will receive are more likely to be recession proof and positive in the long term.

19.5 Looking Ahead: Expanding the Horizon of Ethical Investing

The chapters in this book have traced the core terrain of ethical finance in India, but the conversation around responsible capital continues to grow. For readers who wish to take the next step, the following themes stand out as particularly important for the years ahead.

International Ethical Opportunities: Indian investors can now use the Reserve Bank of India's Liberalised Remittance Scheme to invest up to USD 250,000 per year in overseas markets. This opens doors to global ESG index funds and thematic exchange-traded funds (ETFs) focusing on renewable energy, clean water and healthcare access. International green bonds and the newer blue bonds, issued by bodies such as the World Bank and the Asian Development Bank, allow savers to earn fixed income while directly financing climate and ocean-protection projects. These vehicles introduce currency and taxation considerations, but they broaden the ethical investor's toolkit beyond national borders.

Philanthropy as an Asset Class: Donating is not merely charity; it is a form of social investment. Planned giving, by setting aside a fixed percentage of income for causes such as education, healthcare or environmental restoration, creates a measurable "social return on investment" (SROI). Tools such as GuideStar India, Give.do and international sites like Charity Navigator help evaluate the governance and impact of NGOs. New vehicles such as Development Impact Bonds (for example, the Educate Girls bond in Rajasthan) repay investors only when social outcomes are achieved, blending giving and investing.

Behavioural Finance and Money Habits: Even the best-designed ethical portfolio can falter if fear or euphoria drives decision-making. Common behavioural biases, such as loss aversion, herding and present bias, often lead to short-term or contradictory choices. Simple "nudges" counteract them: automatic SIPs and donations, default options that favour ESG funds, and a 48-hour cooling-off rule before making large trades. These structures help keep everyday behaviour aligned with long-term ethical intentions.

About the authors

Siva Prasad Bose is an author of introductory guidebooks on aspects of Indian laws. He is currently retired after many years of service as an electrical engineer in Uttar Pradesh Power Corporation Limited. He received his engineering degree from Jadavpur University, Kolkata and has a law degree from Meerut University, Meerut and a BSc from MMH College, Ghaziabad. His interests lie in the fields of family law, civil law, law of contracts, and areas of law related to power electricity related issues. He lives in Delhi.

Joy Bose is a data scientist by profession. He is also qualified as a National Institute of Securities Management (NISM) Certified Mutual Funds Distributor and NISM Certified Investor.

Other Books by Siva Prasad Bose

Introduction to Wills and Probate

Senior Citizens Abuse in India

Introduction to Negotiable Instruments

Introduction to Marriage Laws in India

Neighbor Problems in India and what to do about them

Delays in Court Cases in India

Self-Publish Books and E-Books in India

Introduction to Patents and Patent Law in India

Introduction to Property Law in India

.